BOMBS
TO TRAILS

INTERWEAVING HERITAGE, LIFE, AND PTSD ON THE PACIFIC CREST TRAIL

Jessica Pekari

ISBN: 978-0-578-33888-0

Find more from the author at
http://www.adventuresonthetrail.com

Authors Note:
Mileage is not an exact measurement of where I am on the trail because it includes hiking to and from resupply points as well as areas I had to backtrack.

CHAPTER 1

FLASHBACK

"It's a war within yourself that never goes away."
-Anonymous

BOOM! The loud detonation shakes me to my core. My heart starts racing. The Humvee in front of ours is hit. Minutes later, another IED blasts with a loud bang, followed by a third. Radio communications start blaring, "We've been hit. We need Doc." I reach over and grab my aid bag, rifle in hand. Our convoy does their best to push out of the kill zone and into a fairly safe place. It's just enough for me to exit. The Humvees circle me, each facing out, keeping watch. I exit the vehicle hovering as low as I possibly can get to the ground.

Inside the Humvee, the gunner, a Specialist, is still conscious and laid out flat on the floor. He says, "I saw him. I saw the man who pulled the trigger." I tell him to lay still, that everything will be alright. I ask several questions while searching for injuries. I perform a blood sweep, check his pupils and airway. Everything looks normal, but in my gut, I know something isn't right. He is not acting like himself. I reach into my leg pouch, pull out an IV kit, and quickly stick his arm with an 18-gauge needle.

Our convoy commander, a Staff Sergeant, makes his way towards me. "Do we need a medevac?"

"Yes!" I scream. I place a c-collar carefully around his neck. Two more soldiers exit their vehicles to help. I tell one of them to grab the litter. We carefully position the Specialist onto it. I yell at the top of my lungs, "Where is the Medevac?"

"No one is responding," shouts the convoy commander.

"How close are we to the next base?" He tells me it's eight miles. "Okay," I say. "Let's go."

The soldiers help load our wounded friend into the back of the Humvee. The litter barely fits, but we make it work. I enter, kneeling between the driver and passenger seat where our convoy commander sits. While connecting him to a bag of fluids, I continue asking the Specialist questions: what day is it; how are you; what is your name? Moments later, he tells me I sound like Charlie Brown's teacher and loses consciousness.

"How much further!?" I yell.

"Just a few more minutes," the Staff Sergeant responds.

These minutes feel like hours. Time has slowed. I have never felt so helpless, and I hate it. It's just him and me. His life is in my hands. I continue searching, trying to check off everything that may be wrong with him in my head. Everything I have learned from my training. It has to be internal. Something I can't see, but what is it? I rub his sternum to wake him, but there's no response. His eyes don't react to the light I flash over them. I check for a pulse; it is barely there. I look at his chest, no rise and fall. *He needs air*, I tell myself. I begin mouth-to-mouth resuscitation. After three breaths, he starts convulsing. I try to breathe for him again. And just as I start to yell, "How much further," we are in front of the medical building. Soldiers open the Humvee's door. I grab one side of the litter, and we rush him inside.

My husband's voice telling the kids to get ready breaks me out of my trance. I take a deep breath. Just another flashback.

CHAPTER 2

SAYING GOODBYE

"Behind every strong soldier, there is an even stronger
family who stands by them, supports them, and loves
them with all their heart"

-Anonymous

THE KIDS PILE INTO THE BACKSEAT OF MY CAR. It is a short drive to
the airport for the moment we have been dreading all year. Tim
is deploying to Africa. He is leaving today for an unknown
amount of time. He has been deployed or has had to go away
for training before, but this time feels different. The kids are
older and more aware when he's gone. We spent the morning
hanging out and enjoying our last hours together. From the Colorado Springs airport, we will leave for Washington State. The
car is filled with sorrow as we make the drive to drop him off.

I pull into the departure lane and park the car. Tim kisses
me. As he steps out, his six-foot-two frame hovers over my
small car. Just like most soldiers, his light brown hair is short,
and he's clean-shaven. Tim opens the door for our 10-year-old
son, TJ, short for Tennessee James. TJ is our oldest of three. He
brushes back his long, shaggy hair and turns to hug his father
goodbye. Both he and Tim are so much alike, sharing the same
serious and stern look.

4

Tim then reaches over to hug and kiss our seven- and eight-year-old girls on the cheeks. Carolynn and Julianna are the same height with long, brown hair. People often mistake them for twins because they are only an inch apart.

Tim slowly closes their door, grabs his bags, and pets our two dogs on the head. As he waves goodbye, our youngest daughter starts to tear up. They yell, "I love you, daddy," from the car window, blow kisses, and we slowly drive away. I look through my rearview mirror, taking one last look at my husband, and then glance at the sad looks on our children's faces.

Our youngest daughter grasps tightly onto her daddy soldier doll given to her during his last deployment. She lugs that thing around everywhere. Although Tim has left before because of training or deployments, it never gets easier. The older our kids get, the more difficult deployments become for them. They have a better grasp of time and an even greater understanding of what deployments genuinely mean.

The children know their dad is a soldier in the Army who takes care of the sick and wounded, but deployments mean time away from him. It means birthdays and holidays missed, and no hugs or kisses from him at night. I know it cannot be easy being a military child, and I do my best to comfort them. I tell them that time will go by fast, and before we know it, he will be back. I tell them they can still message him whenever they want, and he will respond as soon as he can. I cheer them up by asking what song they would like to hear on the radio. They all agree on "Shake It Off" by Taylor Swift.

CHAPTER 3

ROAD TRIP

"Life is just what it is—a long road trip that sometimes has bumps and sometimes doesn't. Either way, you just gotta keep rollin' along."

-Rebecca Hollard

WE HAVE A LONG ROAD TRIP ahead of us. I am driving my green Subaru Outback, and every inch of it is packed full of hiking gear and Pacific Crest Trail (PCT) resupply boxes. Our two big dogs, Roxy, a twelve-year-old Labrador, and Lily, a three-year-old Weimaraner, are also buckled into the back of the car. There is a cargo box on top of the car with even more Pacific Crest Trail resupply boxes. They are the large flat rate boxes from the United States Postal Service, ten total. Each box contains items I will need along the trail, like new shoes, food, clothing, and toiletries. Once I make it to Washington, I will mail the boxes to predetermined locations on the trail. Next to the cargo box is a black cargo bag full of clothes my children will need for the summer. The cargo bag helps provide more space for our dogs in the back of the car.

We have a two-day journey ahead of us to make it to Washington State. Since I will be on the PCT, my kids will be staying with my mom and sister Glenna and her wife, Yasmin, for the summer. Although they will miss their dad and me, they are excited about the adventure. Having them stay in Washington is also the perfect location to see them once or twice along my hiking route.

Guilt constantly crosses my mind, and I feel like a terrible mother. I love my kids dearly, and when I first started prepping for my hike, their dad deploying was not supposed to be part of the plan. Once we found out he would be gone for at least six months, I wanted to cancel my hike. I discussed my feelings with Tim, and he told me we would find a way where the kids would be taken care of and I could still hike. As usual, he was highly supportive and logical. Although hesitant throughout a lot of back and forth with Tim, I finally decided to continue packing and planning for the PCT thanks to his support. We would talk with my family about the possibility of our kids spending the summer with them. Luckily, they were ecstatic for our kids to visit and started planning for summer adventures almost immediately.

The Pacific Crest Trail was something I had wanted to do for almost ten years. Ever since my husband joined our friend Adam Sumner on the Appalachian Trail in 2010, I had started researching different thru-hikes. My husband told me about the Pacific Crest Trail and how it traversed through California, Oregon, and Washington State. From that point on, a dream had blossomed. At that time, our son was only a few months old. So, I placed the idea into the far regions of my mind hoping that maybe one day I could live out that dream. Life went on. I got out of the Army. I used my G.I. Bill to finish my Bachelor's of Science in Sports and Health Sciences and my Master's of Art in Physical Education. I earned my teaching certification in both physical and special education. We had three kids and moved around the world from one duty station to the next, from North Carolina to Germany to Texas, and finally to where we live now, Colorado.

I started running ultramarathons in 2015 in the Franklin Mountains of El Paso, Texas. Ever since, my love for long treks grew, and I was soon running 200-mile ultras. In 2018, I registered for the Triple Crown of 200s. This included three 200-mile races held in Washington, Nevada, and Utah. All the races took place within a month from each other. For the female division, I placed second at the Bigfoot 200 in Washington State, fourth at the Tahoe 200 in Nevada, and first at the Moab 240 in Utah. I was also the overall winner for the women's Triple Crown category.

It was not until 2019 that my husband and I decided that 2020 would be the perfect year for me to hike the PCT, or so I thought. With almost twenty hours of driving ahead, I take time to reflect on everything that has led to this moment.

I could have chosen to hike the Pacific Crest Trail at a leisurely pace, but I wanted a new challenge. I enjoyed the longer ultras and pushing my body to its limits. I have three kids, and trying to finish the trail as soon as possible to get back to them is just the motivation I needed.

With the support of my husband, I started researching Fastest Known Time (FKT) records for the Pacific Crest Trail. While researching, I learned the interesting story of the trail's beginnings.

For instance, founder Clinton C. Clarke had pushed for the creation of the trail in the 1930s but creating a 2,650-mile trail seemed unfathomable at the time. With the help of co-founders Catherine Montgomery, Fred Cleator, and Warren Rogers, they eventually finished the trail. Cleator mapped the route of the Oregon Skyline Trail. Montgomery proposed the trail to run through Washington, Oregon, and California. Rogers helped scout the route. With these four brilliant minds, trail building began in 1932. It wasn't until 1993 that construction finished. Since then, about 700 to 800 hikers attempt to complete the PCT each year, most heading in a traditional northbound direction. With the trail's completion, many hikers began setting and breaking several records heading northbound (NOBO) from the Mexican border to the Canadian border.

Although many people have set records hiking NOBO, heading southbound (SOBO) in the opposite direction is different. I learned no woman has set a PCT Southbound Fastest Known Time record. Look at the Fastest Known Time website for current Pacific Crest Trail record-holders heading southbound, and you will only see one name: Scott Williamson. He set the record on October 11, 2011, in 64 days, 11 hours, and 19 minutes. Since he did it self-supported, I wanted to follow in his footsteps. Thru-hikers can set a few different types of records. Basically, an unsupported record means you carry everything. A supported record means people can help you. By choosing self-supported, no pre-arrangements can be made with others when it comes to supplying me with food or aid. I can pre-mail food packages and buy food from stores en route, so long as I hike to and from those locations on foot. Unsupported also means car rides are out of the picture.

To beat Williamson's record, I will have to abide by all these rules and average almost forty-two miles a day. Aiming for the record using the Southbound FKT route means starting the hike near the Canadian border and finishing near the Mexican border, or 2,650 miles. However, starting from the Northern Terminus requires an additional thirty miles because, according to the FKT route rules, a hiker can only legally cross the border with proper documentation on foot. Reaching the starting point at Manning Park by car is not allowed. The additional thirty-mile difference can add two days or more to the hike, which is a significant difference when aiming to set a new record.

Given the extra thirty miles, I am not sure why I am so set on heading Southbound. I think it makes sense logistically. My family lives in Washington, which makes planning easier. I can drive from Colorado and stay with my sister until the trail becomes safe enough to hike. I will also have a ride to the start of the trail, and my family can join me for the first thirty miles until I reach the Northern Terminus.

Adding to the stress, just months before starting my hike, the world succumbs to the deadly Coronavirus (COVID-19). Initially, I planned to hike the trail with an ultra-running friend. However, because of the pandemic, she has decided she will wait until there is an improvement with COVID-19 concerns.

The PCT Facebook pages at this time are littered with mixed emotions towards hiking during a pandemic. Comments like "Just stay home" or "It's safer being on the trail" are equally met with backlash. Hikers are bullying each other, making others even more apprehensive about posting anything about the PCT. Any mention of hiking during the pandemic often leads to heated online discussions. Because of such backlash, Facebook members created an additional Facebook page called "Still Hiking PCT Class of 2020." Here, hikers find a positive place to talk about the trail. Hikers discuss information regarding the PCT on this page without worrying about the negativity of those who are against it during the pandemic. The truth is, the virus is new. No one knows where the year will lead or what the future holds. It may even be a few years before permits are reissued.

What we do know is that, unlike previous years, the trail will be different. There will be far fewer hikers attempting to complete the trail this year. I learned that the several places hikers typically send resupply boxes will be closed for the season because of COVID-19. I have no choice but to carry more food with me for longer distances. And still, the possibility exists that I may reach a planned resupply point only to find it shut down due to health concerns.

I respect the new virus and will take the necessary precautions when hiking near others, including walking to and from town. I will wear a face mask when needed, maintain the recommended six feet apart from others, and hand sanitizer will become my best friend.

My past deployments changed my perspective on life. I don't know what the future holds, and we are never guaranteed a tomorrow. However, I won't waste this opportunity of a lifetime I have been given, and if I don't take my chance, I will live with regret. I know the odds are stacked against me, but I am used to challenges and welcome whatever obstacles lie ahead.

CHAPTER 4

"Carry as little as possible,
but choose that little with care."

-Earl Shaffer

I SLOWLY BOUGHT THE NECESSARY GEAR over the few months leading up to my hike. I quickly learned that the lighter the gear, the greater the cost. I tried my best to get the lightest gear possible without breaking the bank. With the help of my ultrarunning friend, we emailed companies in hopes of gaining sponsorships. Luckily, Zpacks hooked me up with the Nero 38L backpack. It is not only comfortable but also weighs less than a pound. Silverstar Nutrition provided as much protein powder and electrolytes as needed for the trail. Trail Toes gave me packets of their cream, which helps aid in the prevention of blisters and chafe. I had fallen in love with the taste of PERC Coffee before hitting the trail, so I emailed them. In return, they provided me with enough packets of instant coffee to keep me energized and going for the next sixty-plus days.

I also had the support of my running team, Trail Racing Over Texas. Rob and Rachel Goyen, the race directors, were highly supportive and told me to message them should I need anything mailed to me along the way. Since moving to Colorado, I was

13

only teaching online in the mornings, which gave me plenty of time to hike, gather gear, and prepare. I became obsessed with learning as much as possible about backpacking, equipment, food, and the trail. For almost a year, not a day went by where I hadn't listened to an audiobook, watched a YouTube video, or read a blog about the PCT.

I spent months gathering enough food for my resupply boxes. My dehydrator ran nonstop for weeks. I even dehydrated ground Oryx meat from my husband's hunt in White Sands, New Mexico, earlier that year. The meat comes from the African antelope and tastes like grass-fed beef.

I picked fellow hiker Adam Sumner's brain, and his mother, Lisa, gave me recipes and tips for what types of foods taste great and rehydrate well. I experimented with dehydrated food, and my kids were there to taste-test everything. If you want an honest opinion about taste, ask a child. My kids enjoyed the taste of dehydrated apples. Still, they told me my rehydrated taco meat was the worst thing they had ever eaten. They were right; it tasted awful. Their complaints caused me to go back to the drawing board and figure out how to improve the taste. Adding more seasoning seemed to do the trick.

I ran several virtual races in my neighborhood organized by Trail Racing Over Texas to prepare for the long distances I would face every day. I completed most of the races wearing my fully loaded Zpacks hiking pack. I wore a twenty-five-pound vest daily, first starting with thirty minutes and working my way up to the entire day. I spent the year focusing more on hiking with my pack than I did with my favorite sport, long-distance running.

I was in a zone, recalling what other types of training I have done to prepare, when a loud bang from the car's rooftop breaks me away from my thoughts. We've made it to Wyoming, and the wind has picked up. Again, I hear a loud noise on the top of my Subaru. We are going eighty miles per hour, but it feels like everything is happening in slow motion. I look out my rearview window and see my trail shoe flying away from my car along with one of my precious PCT boxes. A semi-truck trails us, and my box and shoe hit its grate, smashing into a million pieces. My eyes widen in disbelief. As soon as I can, I pull off the road. I hop out and run to the side of my car. I cannot believe what just happened. As I look up, my cargo box lid has managed to come unlocked, banging itself to the roof bag on my car as it opens and closes in the wind. I open the passenger door, step up onto the seat, and raise myself to get a better glimpse at what I may have just lost.

My kids start drilling me with all kinds of questions at once. *What are you doing, mom? What is happening? Why did we stop? Is everything okay?*

My heart rate increases as I count my boxes: one, two, three, four, five, six. *Okay, phew, it was only that one box. Not too bad,* I tell myself, *only one box and one shoe.* It could be much worse. I explain to my kids what happened as I try to re-latch my cargo box. I get back in my car and buckle up in dismay. I pull out my phone and open a spreadsheet I have showing me what each box contains. I quickly glance over it. *Good, nothing of great value, only food.*

I take the next exit. If I go back to where I lost my box, maybe I can salvage my shoe and some of the items I just lost. As I drive by where my box became a flying projectile, I realize the hopelessness of this effort. The high speed limit makes it unsafe to try and retrieve any items that are on the road. So, I shift my gaze toward the far side of the land just off the road. I notice my shoe has been pushed far off into some shrubs. I quickly run over and grab it. It now has a hole on the side of it with black scuff marks all around. I can spot my empty PCT box ten feet off the road. I grab it and fumble to fold it back to a box-like shape. I also see wrappers and broken food packages near it. Nothing is in usable condition. I do my best to pick up all of the litter I created by stuffing everything into my broken box.

I return to my car. I climb back onto the passenger seat, reach for the rest of my PCT boxes that are still in my cargo box, and start handing them down to my kids. My kids help stack them on the front seat and below their feet. They look like a bunch of sardines but don't complain. Moving the boxes inside the car was a smart choice because although I re-latch the cargo box, it flings open again soon after we are back on the road. I pull over to fix it, but it's pointless. The cargo box continues to re-open.

Just at the right time, my husband calls. He has arrived at his next destination and calls while waiting for his next flight. I tell him what happened, and he tells me to secure it with a bungee cord, which I should be able to buy at the next gas station.

I drive off, and once again, the cargo lid swings open. After stopping a few more pointless times, it continues to re-open, so I give up and decide to let it sway in the wind until I reach the nearest gas station. I enter the store to buy duct tape and bungee cords. I also buy everyone an ice cream bar. When I return to the car, I bungee the cargo box lid shut and surround it with duct tape until I'm satisfied there is no way it can open. We continue our drive hoping to make it safely and without incident to my sister's house.

CHAPTER 5

SETTING OFF

"Don't wait. The time will never be just right."

-Napoleon Hill

I FINALLY REACH MY SISTER'S HOUSE in Washington, but I must wait a few weeks before starting my hike since my permit start date isn't until the end of the month. When the day of my hike finally arrives, the trail conditions from Hart's Pass are considered unsafe. My sister drives with me to the trailhead to scope it out, and we agree that it is just not safe to start. I decide to push back my hike by a few days.

I continue to monitor the PCT Facebook pages for trail conditions and any information regarding the beginning sections of the trail. According to one of the pages, snow still covers much of the ground. Although there are a few alternate routes, no one has posted anything about making it to the Northern Terminus via the PCT route. To attempt a Southbound Fastest Known Time record, I must follow the official Pacific Crest Trail route. Following the record rules means no detours, unless the original route has been closed and rerouted.

Eager to start the trail after a few days, I realize the snow isn't going anywhere. As a safety measure, I order an ice axe and crampons. Maybe the trail is not as bad as hikers are saying. What may be overwhelming to one person, may not be as overwhelming to another. I am highly optimistic and in a time crunch. My kids will go back to school in the middle of August, and I need to make it back in time for their return. From here on, I have to make smart and safe decisions.

If I start the hike and the conditions are unsafe, I can return and postpone for one more week. After that, I will have no chance of making it back home in time. No one has posted about the hike to the Monument from the PCT route. I haven't read any updates on the Facebook page about the trail heading further southbound from Hart's Pass because no one in the group had recently hiked these snow-covered sections. Most hikers have decided to start later in the month or skip ahead and come back later to complete what they have missed. Since I am attempting the Southbound FKT, skipping ahead is not an option. For me, this means hiking without knowing anything about the trail conditions. I will have to hike exactly from one point to the next without skipping any sections.

A few months before the start of my hike, my brother Michael, cousin Kevin, and sister Glenna decided to join me for the first thirty miles to the Northern Terminus. After that, I would start my FKT attempt and set off on my own. Once I told my family about my decision to start, my brother and cousin agreed to meet at my sister's house the day before our departure, where we would further discuss our plans for the hike.

Since I am already packed and ready to hit the trail, we spend the night doing gear layouts for my cousin Kevin, brother, and sister. We want to make sure everyone has what they need for the next few days of backpacking. I bring my husband's micro-spikes and let my cousin borrow them. I also tell him he can borrow my extra zero-degree sleeping bag. He agrees to try it out, so he lays down and gets inside of it. We all start to laugh as he tries to pull up the bag towards his head. But my cousin is tall and skinny, and the sleeping bag only reaches the navel of his extra-long six-foot-six frame. As previously planned, my brother lets him use his extra, better-fitting sleeping bag since they have very similar body types and height.

We sit around and talk about our previous failed adventure earlier in the year. Time has passed, and we have all healed from it, allowing laughter to lead the storytelling. I had regis-tered for a 200-mile ultra. This is a distance that I have been successful at multiple times and have grown to love. It would be my second year in a row running the Franklin Mountain 200 miler put on by Trail Racing Over Texas. My sister had regis-tered for the 200k, and my brother and cousin registered for the shorter 100k distance, where they would stick together. Feeling overconfident and wanting to push limits even further, I also registered for the 100k. I planned to finish the 200 miles, sleep, and then hike and run the 100k with my brother and cousin.

I spent months training, and on the day of the race, I felt strong. After the second loop and a 100k in, I was in second place, trailing the lead runner by only a few miles. I was excited to be chasing such a phenomenal athlete. It had snowed that morning and continued to be a chilly day. My hydration pack straw froze, so I stopped drinking water and focused on only consuming the electrolytes from the extra water bottle on the front of my hydration vest. This misfortune is where things took a turn for the worst. Not realizing that I had not been drinking water that day and only electrolytes, my body began to shut down. I had severe cramping in my legs, but I figured it was from the long distance I had just tackled.

The course is composed of loops. The most challenging section is a climb up to the North Peak. A 2,000-foot climb once you left the start/finish aid station. Once I reached that aid station, I took some Tylenol in hopes it would take away the pain from my legs. It did nothing. My body did not process the Tylenol, and my legs continued to cramp and ache. Having pain medication not help with aches had never happened to me before.

It was a slow hike up towards the next aid station called Mundys Gap. After this point, it is an out and back to the peak. So, I topped off my extra bottle with more electrolytes and took a swig of water, only it was too late. Pushing through the pain and being optimistic, I continued. I made it to the peak for a third time, but the pressure on my legs continued to get worse hiking down. I took a seat and rested a few minutes before continuing. I battled with myself for the next thirty minutes until I reached the Mundys Gap aid station once again.

Another trail runner, Erin, who was volunteering at the Mundys Gap aid station, asked how I was doing. I told her what I was feeling and knew I didn't have it in me to make it to the next aid station. I decided to hike back down towards the start/finish area. Maybe I could sleep and feel better. Up to this point, I had been awake for over thirty hours and had finished 100 miles of this grueling course. Erin agreed to hike down with me. We made it a half-mile, and I stopped to rest again. Only this time, I called my mom and asked if she could pick me up at the base of the mountain. Staying in a nearby Airbnb, she arrived within minutes.

Once my friend and I made it to the truck, my brother helped me get inside. I lay across the seats, but shook uncontrollably with pain. We stopped at a nearby drive-thru for food and soda, but these were the last things on my mind. I told my mom to drive straight to the hospital. After I entered the hospital and was examined by a nurse, I was given a urinalysis cup. But in the bathroom, my heart sank within seconds. My urine was the color of Coca-Cola. The hospital staff admitted me immediately, and I learned I had rhabdomyolysis.

Rhabdomyolysis occurs when your body is overworked, causing your muscles to rupture. The damaged muscle cells leak into the bloodstream, which can lead to severe complications, such as kidney damage. People with rhabdomyolysis can avoid major complications if diagnosed early, and normal exercise can resume within a few months, or even within a few weeks in some cases. Since electrolyte abnormalities are prominent features of rhabdomyolysis, consuming mostly electrolytes during my race actually further hurt my muscles.

I spent the next five days being pumped with fluids and waiting in the hospital for my blood work to return somewhat normal. My sister forced herself to stop one loop shy of finishing 200k. Her face experienced swelling after some type of allergic reaction.

My brother and cousin stopped after one loop. It was a first for them, so they were happy with their accomplishment. We all went away without even one of us completing the distances we set out to do. I learned a valuable lesson; from that point on, I vowed to drink a cup of water every morning to start my day.

As we sit in my sister's garage with our dark and twisted humor, we begin to make fun of each other's Franklin Mountain race failures. We laugh at how my sister's lips were so swollen it looked like she had a terrible Botox job. We tease my cousin for posting a video on the first loop about how easy it was and how he was going to go away with the 100k buckle. We laugh about the race. You climb, thinking the entire time you will soon get a nice downhill, only to turn the corner and come face-to-face with more climbing. We even crack a joke about my cousin's face when he first showed up in El Paso to visit me in the hospital. His 100k didn't start until three days after my race. The last thing anyone wants to see before going into their first ultra is a family member in the hospital because of it.

It is getting late. We all decide it is time to go to sleep. I lie in bed tossing and turning, excited for tomorrow.

We greet the morning with the smell of delicious bacon. My mom has cooked us all breakfast. While eating, I receive an email. Although my ice axe has yet to arrive, the crampons I had ordered earlier in the week are ready for in-store pickup. I also schedule a meeting with a notary to sign papers on refinancing our home. I was supposed to meet with her the day prior but with COVID-19, getting a notary to meet is difficult. So, I had to wait an extra day. Since the notary cannot meet until the afternoon, we take our time loading gear in the trucks. The waiting also gives me spare time to spend with my kids.

I want to forgo signing. It took weeks for the company to gather the proper paperwork. The timing can not have been any more inconvenient. I know it is necessary, so we all agree to leave as soon as I finish signing. Luckily, the lady meets us in the parking lot where I need to pick up my crampons.

Once I finish signing the paperwork, I head inside to pick up my gear order. I learn my ice axe has still not arrived. I will have to settle for buying a heavier one. I think about not buying one at all, but I know I may need it. There are not many ice axes to choose from and all are much heavier than I want. Once I decide on one, I get in line. While waiting for my turn to check out, I glance over and notice a pile of boxes on a cart. In giant black letters, one of the boxes has my last name, PEKARI, written on it. I get excited. That is my ice axe! I speak with the cashier, and she goes over to retrieve it. She brings it to the cash register and lets me open it up. "Perfect," I say out loud gleefully. "Simply perfect." *So light and easy to handle*. The cashier smiles. I exit the store, returning to the truck enthusiastically, telling my family what has just happened. We can finally leave for the trail.

The drive is three hours long, and it is almost two in the afternoon. If I delay my start date another day, my brother cannot join us. We take separate vehicles since he will have to return for work after the first night of camping. My sister and I ride in her truck while my cousin and brother ride in another. We are a few hours into our drive, and my thoughts start to stray toward the trail once again. There are so many unknowns. *How will the trail conditions be once we are out there? What obstacles will I have to overcome? How will my body react to all the miles I have planned for it?* The questions I have running through my mind are endless. But, I have not begun to share my thoughts or feelings with anyone. I have always been the type to keep my feelings and emotions bottled up.

I continue to gaze out of the passenger window and try not to think about how nervous I am. Then something catches my eye: a beautiful bald eagle perched atop a fence. Suddenly, my nerves have calmed as my thoughts shift toward the animal. I cannot recall how many eagles I have seen roaming freely in my lifetime, but I know it is not very many. Glenna glances towards it and chuckles at my excitement.

My siblings and I were raised around three different cultures. Our step-father is Filipino, born and raised in the Philippines. Our mother is Blackfeet Indian, and grew up on the reservation in Browning, Montana. Our father was raised in the State of Mexico near Mexico City. Eagles are sacred in both the Blackfeet and Hispanic cultures, so we share an enduring love and respect for them. I stare out my window, mesmerized by the eagle until my sister's voice brings me back to reality, "I think seeing the Eagle is a sign of good things to come, sis." I nod in agreement, thinking, *I really hope you're right.*

To pass the time on our drive, I discuss my trail bucket list with my sister. I tell her, "I made a list of things I would like to see and do while I am on the trail." Here is what I have so far:

1. Sit and watch the sunrise. Not catch it while I am hiking, but take the time to sit and watch it rise.

2. The same goes for the sunset. Sit and watch it set.

3. Take a dip in a lake.

4. Hike with my kids.

5. See a shooting star.

6. Be above the clouds.

7. There is a philosophical saying, "If a tree falls in a forest and no one is around to hear it, does it make a sound?" I have never seen a tree fall in the woods before, and I would like to see one randomly fall over. From a distance, of course. (My sister gets a kick out of this weird bucket list item.)

8. Eat a large package of Oreos in one day.

9. Eat a large pizza in one day. I haven't been able to do this since high school.

My sister enjoys my list and tries to help me come up with more items. We laugh at her ridiculous suggestions, such as trying a headstand on a rock while juggling.

It is becoming late, but I don't worry. We take our time getting to the trail and make a quick stop for dinner. We order pizza for my last meal before heading off into the wilderness. I order a medium Margherita pizza with a large soda and eat as much of it as possible. Of course, I can't finish it and leave what's left in my sister's truck.

Once we make the final turn onto Hart's Pass, my nerves intensify once more, and I begin shaking my legs, my foot bouncing against the floor of the truck. The drive up to the trailhead is narrow, with long drop-offs on one side of the dirt road. The road was built in 1893 and hangs alongside cliff walls. It gives magnificent views of vistas and canyons. Reaching just over 6,000 feet, it is the highest point anyone can drive in the state of Washington. Luckily, we don't cross paths with any vehicles coming down.

My brother and sister maneuver their way up to the start of the PCT with ease. It is almost six in the evening when we make it to the parking lot near the trailhead, but we don't care. We had talked about getting a room for the night, but we decide to go on with it since we still have a few hours to hike.

WASHINGTON

"The greatest adventure is what lies ahead.
Today and tomorrow are yet to be said.
The chances, the changes are all yours to make.
The mold of your life is in your hands to break."

-JRR Tolkien,
from *The Hobbit*

CHAPTER 6

DAY 1 TO THE NORTHERN TERMINUS

July 1 - 6:05 p.m. (time started)

3.65 miles / 935 feet (mileage and elevation for the day)

2 hours, 15 minutes (time hiked)

"What wonders lie in every mountain day?"

-John Muir

AS WE EXIT OUR VEHICLES, the sun begins to set, and it is cold and drizzly outside. We put ponchos over our packs to help our gear stay dry. We start to hike towards the Northern Monument near Canada.

I am filled with excitement and mixed emotions. I am finally doing it! Months and months of planning have led up to this moment. I feel fortunate and a bit relieved to have my brother, sister, and cousin help ease me into these first few days of hiking.

As we look for the start of the trail, the rain has now turned into big droplets. There it is! My first PCT emblem. It is a curved triangular shape with the color teal on the inside, outlined with white. Inside the teal triangle is a big tree with mountains behind it. Above this picture are the words "Pacific Crest Trail," all in capital letters. Also, in capital letters and below the tree in smaller lettering are the words "NATIONAL SCENIC TRAIL." It is the first of many PCT emblems I will see on my trek. I make a mental note of the symbol as we begin our adventure.

Snow covers the ground in several sections but not enough to use microspikes. I lead the way, trekking as slowly and safely as possible. I plan to take my time the first few days until I hit the Northern Monument. The first mile is a breeze, but then there is a shift in the weather. The temperature drops, and the view becomes obsolete. The rain has now turned into snow, and the wind picks up, smacking the snow heavily into our faces. Visibility is minimal, and I realize that the miles will not come easily. We only make it three miles the first day. We arrive at camp cold but in high spirits. We laugh at the unpredictable weather and that we've only made it three miles. Born and raised in Washington, changing weather is something we have all grown to expect. Hopefully, tomorrow is better, and the trail conditions will have eased.

Still full from the pizza, we munch on beef jerky for dinner. My sister and I share my two-person tent. My brother and cousin volunteer to take our bear bags, and they hang them away from camp. My bear bag is composed of a bulletproof spectral fabric that is supposed to keep bears from getting into it as well as prevent tiny critters like squirrels from entering. I decided to line the inside with an odor-resistant bag in hopes nothing can smell all the deliciousness packed away inside it. Unlike a standard bag where you have to hang it high, these bear bags are made to be tied towards the base of a tree or a lower branch. This will be beneficial when tall trees are sparse and helps to expedite storing food away from camp. Since my family decided on regular bear bags, my cousin and brother hang them together high in a tree.

They arrive moments later and hop into their three-person tent. Once my sister and I are in my tent, we start to set up our gear for the night. I use my pump sack to help Glenna air up her mattress. Then I move on to it alongside her to give myself enough space to air up mine. My tent is not very big but has just enough room for both of us. As I lay my sleeping quilt out, I feel a pop beneath my bottom. "Oh no!" I exclaim. "I think I just put a hole in your sleeping pad, Glenna."

She shrugs her shoulders. "No worries, sis," she says. "It's old anyway." As her air mattress slowly deflates, I apologize and ask if she will be okay. She nods her head yes, climbs inside her sleeping bag, and turns to fall asleep.

I slip inside my silk liner tucked inside of my twenty-degree quilt. It is a thin sheet, shaped like a sleeping bag, and adds an extra five degrees to my quilt. It weighs 3.2 ounces and helps keep my quilt cleaner by creating a barrier between myself and it. My quilt has two straps that cinch around my sleeping pad. It is believed that the underside of a regular sleeping bag does not provide much warmth. By cutting that section out, you can shave a few unnecessary ounces. Strapping the quilt around my sleeping pad also prevents cold drafts from entering. My quilt does have a zipper at the bottom. It does not zip all the way and allows just enough room for my feet to snuggle into it. Once the temperatures rise, I can also turn my quilt into a blanket. The sleeping pad I have chosen is insulated and will keep me warm when temperatures drop near single digits. It comes with a pump sack to quickly air up. I plan to trade it out with a regular sleep mat once I am out of the snow. This won't happen until I reach my second resupply point in Oregon. Altogether, my sleep system weighs 2.9 pounds.

I grab my electronics and place them inside my liner. The cold can drain the batteries quickly, and with the temperature dropping at night, I don't want to risk losing power to anything. This includes my Coros watch, Garmin inReach, SPOT device, two 10,000 mAH power banks, and a headlamp. With extensive research, I decided to carry both the SPOT device and the Garmin inReach. The SPOT Device has impressive battery life. It takes triple-A batteries and won't eat away at my power banks. Although I cannot receive messages, the SPOT can send a preset message I created before starting this hike. It allows my friends and family to track my whereabouts. I set it to ping my location every thirty minutes. I will use it to record the entire distance I am trekking. I am only carrying the Garmin inReach to message family and receive weather updates. It will be off most of the time. Both devices have SOS buttons in case of an emergency. My Coros watch has amazing battery life. My goal is to use it to record the entire distance I am hiking. With my SPOT and Coros watch, I have two devices to record my distance if one should fail or run out of battery life.

I lay there anxious and eager for the night to be over as I doze off. A few hours have passed, and I am awakened by my sister's shivering. I ask how she is doing, and she tells me she is cold. I tell her I will share my mattress with her and that it is really warm. She scoots over, and I turn to my side, trying to give each of us as much space on my mattress as possible. But my mattress is small. We start to laugh because, at this point, we are forced to spoon to fit. Then my sister cracks a joke: "Never have I ever had to spoon with my sister." We both start to giggle. Although challenging, I do my best to sleep as still as possible because it causes the other person to wake every time one of us moves. I am uncomfortable, but it is a fair price to pay for both of us to keep warm. After all, it is my fault her air mattress is busted. I doubt not having to share my sleep pad would have done much for me anyway. It wouldn't matter if I were on the most luxurious bed known to mankind. I would have still slept terribly, tossing and turning from excitement and nervousness for tomorrow.

CHAPTER 7

DAY 2 TO THE NORTHERN TERMINUS

July 2 - 10:03 a.m.

13.6 miles / 2,654 feet

8 hours, 33 minutes

"Home is behind you. The world is ahead."
-Gandalf, from J.R.R. Tolkien's
The Fellowship of the Ring

THE FOLLOWING MORNING ARRIVES, and we have dark circles under our eyes. We are used to roughing it, though. Dozens of ultramarathons and our combined military years have given me and my siblings thick skin. We know what it is like to suffer, and last night was far from it. We have been through worse.

For my cousin, Kevin, last night was a first. He has never backpacked before. He complains very little, even though he froze last night. My brother, Michael, gave him hand warmers, but they did very little in keeping him from having a good night's sleep. He tells us that he had to go to the bathroom in the middle of the night but didn't want to go alone. He waited until

35

the morning once my brother was awake and the sun had risen. Our cousin is tough, but this is something he has never experienced before. He wants to continue on with my sister and me, but he also wants to return to the truck with my brother later in the day. Michael quickly helps to change his mind and tells my cousin he just needs the right kind of equipment. He offers Kevin all of his gear, including his hiking boots. He also gives our sister his sleeping pad.

It is a slow start to our morning. No one wanted to leave their sleeping bag's cozy warmth. Glenna and I decide on biscuits and gravy for breakfast. I use my stove to boil water for our dehydrated meals and instant coffee from PERC. Both are delicious and just what we need to get us moving. We take our time eating, enjoying every single bite and sip. We slowly pack up and don't start hiking until ten in the morning.

As we continue our hike over Buffalo Pass, we are surprised by the views. Yesterday's visibility was so minimal and cold. Today feels as though we have traveled to a different place in the world. The sky is clear, and the sun is out. I close my eyes and turn my head towards the sun, soaking in the warmth of its gentle rays. I open my eyes and look off into the distance. There are patches of snow everywhere. Evergreens cover the landscape, giving off the sweet smell of pine. We hike a quarter of a mile and stop near a stream to fill up our water bottles. The water is ice cold and refreshing.

As we sit there drinking, we all smile at a deer lying near the trail just ahead. Even as we continue on and hike closer, it stays lying in the grass, unbothered by our presence. My brother takes out his phone, snaps a picture, and we trek on. It doesn't last long, though. A quarter of a mile past the deer, we are suddenly halted by a strange noise. We all listen intently as the sound intensifies. It sounds like mini helicopters coming from the nearby tree. As we make our way closer, we see what causes the sound. There are three giant birds perched atop the tree's branches. As the birds work their way to the trail's far side away from us, we stand in awe.

Even with all of our stops admiring nature, we maintain a comfortable and steady pace. We pass another hiker heading back to Hart's Pass from the trail. He tells us he had turned around at Windy Pass, which is less than a mile from us. He tells us that it is snow-covered, and he felt uncomfortable crossing, so he turned back. We keep hiking to see for ourselves.

The hiker was not lying. This section of the trail is on a steep mountainside and does not see much sun. We know many have crossed successfully because shoe imprints are pressed into the snow, leading from the start of this section to the end. Once we reach Windy Pass, we take our time putting on microspikes for better traction. There are several trees at the beginning, so we do our best to maneuver around them. I look back at my sister, and I can see the nervousness on her face. She has never done anything like this before, nor has my cousin. Our pace slows dramatically. We make it past a dozen trees and reach a patch of rocks. With my brother right behind me, we wait for my sister and cousin to catch up. The mountain's angle has become steeper. Uncomfortable with continuing, my sister decides that she will turn back. Not wanting to leave her alone, my cousin turns back with her. My brother, though, has a lot of experience with this type of terrain. He has hiked in much worse. He agrees to continue hiking with me to see how conditions will be for making it over this pass. He tells me that he can hike a few more hours with me since he doesn't have to be back to work until tomorrow. Glenna and Kevin make plans to wait for him in the same location we had camped the night before. My cousin and sister wish me good luck as I hug them goodbye.

My brother and I start the 300-foot climb to the top of the pass. Once we reach the top, we follow the tracks of hikers who set out before us. They lead us in the wrong direction forcing us to turn back and search for a safe way down. My brother soon spots another set of tracks. They zig-zag down the mountain.

I pull out my phone and look at my Guthook guide to make sure we are going the right way this time. This guide is fantastic. I can use it while in airplane mode to conserve my phone's battery life. Guthook allows hikers, such as myself, to input up-to-date trail information. It also has trail and campsite conditions, the direction of the trail, altitude, miles hiked, miles to the nearest campsite, water points, and much more. Although I have a printed-out map, I will lean heavily on this guide.

We move slowly, working our way down and in step with the tracks. We make it down successfully. Two hours have now passed since leaving Glenna and Kevin, and the time has come for my brother to turn back around. Although hesitant, he gives me a big hug and whispers words of advice in my ear. He wishes me good luck and hikes away. I continue to hike, stopping every few feet to look back up toward him until he is no longer visible. He has made it back over the pass. I wonder when I will see him again, when I will see my sister again, and when I will see my kids again.

From this point, snow continues to cover the trail, making it challenging to follow. I wish this section were easier, but the mountain and nature have plans of their own. The mountain does not let you through willingly; you have to work to earn your passage.

I am constantly checking my Guthook guide to ensure I am going in the right direction. I soon approach a section not covered in snow where a female hiker is just beginning to lay out her gear to dry in the sun. I stop to chat with her for a minute and learn that there is another pass further up where she had turned back. It is almost fifteen miles before reaching the Northern Monument. She tells me she has come across other hikers heading that way and wishes me luck. Within minutes of leaving her, I come across two female hikers and a dog. They tell me they, too, had turned around just ahead. An hour later, I cross paths with another group of hikers. They also share the same story. That Rock Pass is impassable. Huge snow cornices have overtaken the rim, making it impossible and dangerous to cross. A man from the group tells me to go check for myself before deciding to turn around. "Who knows," he says, "it may have melted enough to let you pass."

I think he knew; I just needed to see for myself. One of the females tells me, "Not a bad place to start your southbound hike." But they don't know my plans for attempting a Southbound FKT, and I don't bother to tell them. If I skip sections, my attempt will be off.

As I continue my hike towards Rock Pass, I am met with patches of snow along the way. I take off my microspikes when hiking on bare land but find myself having to put them back on when approaching more snow. I grew tired of putting them on, taking them off, and finally decide to keep them on. I have hiked thirteen and one-half miles today. My shoes are soaked from crossing streams and stepping in snow. It is nine in the evening by the time I make it to camp near Rock Pass; everyone else I have talked with today turned back around once they faced it. The sunlight slowly disappears. I dare not attempt to cross it so late in the evening. I camp nearly a mile before the pass at the nearest campsite before reaching Rock Pass. I will check the trail conditions in the morning once I am well-rested. I take time trying to find a suitable place for camping. There are several dead trees around that are still upright, called snags, and I definitely don't want to be pancaked by one. After I find a comfortable place, I set up my tent, make dinner, sit back, and enjoy my surroundings.

When I am finished, I find a tree off in the distance to tie up my bear bag and then return to my tent. Once tucked away inside my sleeping quilt, I message my husband, sister, and mother on my Garmin inReach. I let them all know about the situation for Rock Pass. My sister agrees that she and Kevin will not leave Hart's Pass until I let them know if I have turned back around or decided to press on. Thoughts of Rock Pass run through my mind as I begin to doze off. I'm really hoping I can easily find a safe passage over the pass tomorrow. I really don't want to delay my hike another week or have to re-hike this section all over again. But if I have to, I will. By a quarter to ten that night, I am sound asleep.

CHAPTER 8

DAY 3 TO THE NORTHERN TERMINUS

July 3 - 9:16 a.m.

15.13 miles / 2,231 feet

11 hours, 8 minutes

"Slow is smooth, smooth is fast."

-Anonymous

I WAKE UP FULL OF ENERGY. I have roughly fifteen miles to go today to make it to the Northern Terminus. I sleep in and take my time getting ready. I am less than a mile from Rock Pass and have no idea what lies ahead.

When I retrieve my bear bag, I have a solid breakfast of oatmeal, pound cake, and PERC Coffee. I set aside my food for the day: tortillas and hazelnut for lunch; dehydrated pasta primavera for dinner; Silverstar Nutrition chocolate protein powder; and granola and a few bars for snacks. I pack up the rest of my equipment and start my hike towards Rock Pass.

I reach the snow cornices at Rock Pass in less than a mile. The overhanging mass of hardened snow covers the entire rim, and the trail seems non-existent. I walk around the top of it, following the steps of hikers who have been here before. While looking for a safe passage down, I see nothing. There are no footprints to follow. The only prints I see are of those who have turned back around. I walk back, still searching for a safe route. I see nothing. I continue stepping back and forth near the cornices a few more times, contemplating my next move, and then I see it. There is a safe way down, less than a fifteen-foot drop, where the snow clears. I spend more time thinking things through. I close my eyes and envision what I am about to do. I know that once I make it over, I won't see anyone for days. No one has posted about making it further than this pass. Everyone has turned back around. My stubbornness gets the best of me, and I decide to keep going. For the first time in my life, I strap on crampons and pull out my ice axe. My heart is pounding, but I know I can do this.

I walk to the cliff's edge. I drop to my knees and dig my ice axe into the snow. I slowly lower my body over the edge, crampons kicked into the snow. I begin climbing down, making a ladder pattern to help with my descent. I kick one foot into the snow several times until I am happy with my footing. Then I kick my other foot, stabbing into the snow with my ice axe for support. Within minutes, I make it down safely and onto dry land. I take time to breathe and take in the view. I am really high up, and I can see for miles. Trees upon trees and patches of snow are all that lie ahead.

That wasn't so bad, I tell myself. *It can only get easier from here.* Throughout the day, I must repeatedly kick myself for thinking this as, with each passing hour, things only get more technical.

Although the snow covers much of the trail, I do my best to follow the exact route. I don't want to take any chances that would ruin my Southbound FKT attempt. The descent from Rock Pass is laden with patches of snow. Microspikes are not enough to help me cross its steep, snowy sections.

After hiking a few feet from the crevice, I see snow overtaking the next area. With my ice axe in hand, I drop to my knees and slowly crawl my way across this extremely angled portion of the trail. It zigzags down. I sit down and take my crampons off, thinking I am done with the snow, only to turn the corner to meet more snow patches. Each patch feels as though they are at ninety-degree angles. I know someone has been here before. Faint footprints in the snow disappear almost entirely in the wind and rain. Nonetheless, they are there.

This section would be much easier if the footprints were fresh. I could sink my feet into each of their steps, making it easier and safer for me to press on. Unfortunately, the prints are barely visible. I unhappily wonder when these hikers passed through. I don't know if I will run into anyone any time soon.

I continue, and as I come across each snowy section down from Rock Pass, I make sure to have three points of contact at all times. I place one trekking pole in my pack's mesh and use the other along with my ice axe for balance, giving me a slight sense of security. I soon form a rhythm for these snowy patches. Stab with the ice axe, stab with the trekking pole, and kick two times per foot with my crampons for footing. On some of the steeper snow sections, I stay as low to the ground as possible, often forced to crawl my way across.

The rhythm I have formed suddenly gets thrown off. My right crampon catches the inside of my left pant leg and tears a small hole into it. I trip and fall forward onto my knees. Luckily the snow eases the impact, and I have a solid grasp on my ice axe to keep me from sliding down. I tuck both pants into the straps of the crampons. After I make my way off the snow patch and take a few steps onto the rocky trail, my pants free themselves, and my crampon catches the same pant leg. The crampon tears another giant hole in my pants, causing me to trip and fall to my knees. The rocks dig into my legs, leaving behind some gnarly bruises. Still on the ground, I take a seat. I undo the straps and tuck my pant legs into my socks to prevent myself from falling, but this gives the snow-free access into my shoes. A few snow chunks manage their way in, melting beneath the warmth of my feet.

It takes me an hour to travel a mile. I've completely exhausted myself from crawling my way down from Rock Pass. Why didn't I leave earlier this morning? I have fourteen miles still to go.

Finally, when I have hiked to the bottom, I take my crampons off and replace them with microspikes. The microspikes are less jagged, more comfortable, and a much-needed relief from the heaviness of the crampons. But after a quarter of a mile climb towards the next pass, I am met with nothing but snow and no visible tracks to follow. Feeling on edge, I tell myself, "It's okay, take your time. *Slow is smooth, smooth is fast.*" This phrase was drilled into us when I was in the Army. Sometimes it is quicker to take your time and do the job right rather than trying to move quickly. Rushing could lead to severe mistakes like injury or time-consuming backtracking. So, I take a seat on a nearby rock, take a few deep breaths, and munch some jerky before continuing on.

I make it across Woody Pass with eleven miles left to go for the day, and the trail steepens. Thinking I can traverse it with microspikes, I take a few steps but turn back quickly. I need my more jagged crampons to tackle this section. I sit down and strap my crampons on for what seems like the millionth time today. The clear views I had seen earlier at Rock Pass have now vanished. Fog has overtaken the trail. I have no clue what lies further ahead because I can only see ten feet in front of me now. The footprints I had been following earlier that day are also gone. The wind has taken them back, leaving no trace of their existence. I pull out my phone to double-check which direction to go. I do my best to stay on track and follow the curvature of the mountain. However, like most of today, there is no trail to be seen. Whatever markers laid here years before are now buried deep within the snow. I am on an unmarked, empty slate and forced to backtrack more often than not. I find myself back on my hands and knees, keeping as low to the ground as possible.

The thickening fog has caused my Guthook guide to lag. After backtracking a few more times, I repeat my mantra. *Slow is smooth, smooth is fast.* Just wait for the app to catch up to your location. Once it finally does, I can conserve what little energy I have left for the day and trek on. It takes me seven hours to hike the next nine miles.

The snow finally clears two miles before reaching the Monument. The first mile gives me time to relax. As I make my way down its gradual descent, I tackle the distance in less than thirty minutes. But if there is one thing I learned from the trail so far, it is not to take the easy sections for granted. And just like that, one mile before the Monument, I am met with another obstacle. Trees have fallen everywhere. I knew it would be too early for trail maintenance to be clearing the trail when I started my hike, but I had never imagined the trail to be this rough. In a matter of months, the woods have taken back what is rightfully theirs, and the trail seems almost non-existent.

I scramble to maneuver and climb over the downed trees. My backpack catches and rubs across several of their branches. Some trees are too big to step over, forcing me to pull myself up, crawl underneath, or find a way around. This takes a lot of energy and time. My butt is covered in sap from scooting across the trees. After thirty trees, I soon lose count of how many I have climbed over. Once I am past all of the downed trees, I am met with overgrown shrubs. I weave and bob my way past them. This section should have been easy and fast, but now I'm barely making my day's goal, having to cross all the trees and overgrown bushes.

I make it to the Monument at 8:20 p.m. Although I have seen photos of the Monument before, touching it with my own two hands brings a sense of pride and joy. It is made of five wooden pillars varying in size. The tallest pillar has a giant Pacific Crest Trail emblem mounted to it. The next three are all engraved with the words. The first reads, "NORTHERN TERMINUS PACIFIC CREST NATIONAL SCENIC TRAIL ESTABLISHED BY THE ACT OF CONGRESS ON OCT. 2, 1968." Next to that, another pillar displays the words, "CANADA TO MEXICO 2650 MILES 1988 A.D." And on the smallest pillar, the elevation is engraved, "ELEVATION 4258." Off one of the five pillars hangs a Canadian and American Flag. A canister mounted to the back of the tallest pillar has a logbook inside. I will wait before making an entry. Up until now, I had never thought about what my first PCT entry should read. Setting up camp gives me enough time to really think about what I want to say.

Disappointed it has taken me eleven hours to hike almost fifteen miles, I choose to camp next to the Monument for the night. Surely no one will be hiking this way anytime soon, and I came across zero hikers today. The nearest marked campsite is over three miles back, near Castle Pass. I am also not climbing over those trees more times than I must. I snap a few photos proving that I made it and set up my tent for the night.

After finishing my dinner, I grab the PCT logbook and flip to the SOBO page. I had been trying to decide what I should write for almost an hour. Should I write something meaningful? Perhaps a quote or some fancy saying? Additionally, I have no idea how to explain where I am from originally. Having been in the military and married to an active-duty soldier, I have lived everywhere. My driver's license is from Florida, my license plates are from Texas, and we currently reside in Colorado. Even as a child, I lived in three different cities. After an hour of pondering, I make my first entry simple by writing where we currently reside: Jessica Pekari, Colorado Springs, CO, 7/3/2020. I close the logbook and stare at the PCT emblem on the cover. Months of preparation and hundreds of hours make this feel so surreal. I am filled with an absurd amount of mixed emotions. Excitement, nervousness, anticipation, overwhelmed, and happiness are just a few. I can't believe the start of my FKT attempt is just hours away. I put the logbook back in its big Ziplock bag and place it into the metal ammo case mounted on the Monument. The can is labeled "Northern Terminus Register."

I return to my tent and message my husband on my inReach. I tell him how exhausting today has been. I had no idea I would be battling with so much snow. He suggests that I hang around for another day to have enough energy to start my FKT attempt. I contemplate waiting, but message back that I would be wasting another day of food, and from here, I only have a week's worth. I message my mother, sister, and brother that I have made it and I am excited to start my attempt tomorrow. I fall asleep around ten in the evening and have a solid night of rest.

CHAPTER 9

DAY 1 FKT ATTEMPT

July 4 - 6:50 a.m.

25.58 miles / 6,398 feet

14 hours, 31 minutes

"Food is fuel and fuel is energy."

-Anonymous

MY ALARM GOES OFF AT 6:00 A.M. I lie in bed for a few more minutes mustering up the energy to get up. It's a chilly morning. I slowly put on my hiking clothes and crawl out of my tent. I hike to where my bear bag is and lean against the tree to use the bathroom. Lathering my hands with sanitizer, I reach up and untie my bear bag. I hike back to camp and pull out my breakfast and the rest of the food I'll be eating today. As I boil water for my meal and morning coffee, I pack up everything, placing my stove and propane tank on the side of my pack last. I finish eating and take a few more photos of the Monument.

I can't believe I am about to start my attempt on the Fourth of July. Typically, I spend the day with my kids, who are excited for a firework-filled evening. Unlike others who have served in the military, I have been fortunate not to have fireworks as a PTSD trigger. Instead, lighting fireworks with my family is a sweet memory from my childhood. My mom and dad separated when I was five years old but made it a point to be civil towards one another. We shared holidays with both, which meant double celebrations. Regardless of whose house we were at, we always had fun lighting fireworks. I want my kids to share the same fun memories.

A few days ago, we had a pre-Fourth of July party. My kids and I spent the evening hanging out, making cake, and lighting sparklers. I was also able to see the other fireworks my sister had bought for today's festivity. Both she and my mom had promised to send me personal videos of their reactions to the fireworks. This gives me something to look forward to and helps take my mind off the difficult hike ahead.

Once I've set everything in its proper place, I have to admit, I am a bit nervous. This is it. When I press start on my watch, my FKT attempt begins. The timer keeps going no matter how many breaks I take or stops I make. I take a deep breath, press start on my watch, and video the start of my attempt.

Morning dew covers the shrubs that were dry the previous night. After taking a few steps, my pants become soaked. I should have put my rain pants on. Already soaked, I decide not to bother. I re-climb over all the downed trees ahead. It is just as tricky as the day before. As I scoot my way off of a big tree, the bottom of my pack catches a branch, and I can hear something tear. Once I am on the ground, I remove my backpack to take a look at the damage. There is a four-inch slit at the base. I grab a piece of duct tape from my first aid kit and quickly patch it up.

When I finally make it over and around all of the trees, I begin my ascent up towards Castle Pass, where the snow awaits. I take my time climbing, trying not to be too eager to push my limits just yet. I reach the first campsite from the Monument and suddenly halt. Directly off the trail and on the campsite stands a giant brown bear. It slowly walks in the opposite direction and has yet to notice my presence. Not wanting to startle it, I tap my trekking poles together and continue to walk on the trail in the opposite direction. It glances over at me and continues walking away. I don't want to startle anything that may be in my path, so I spend the next few hours singing cadence.

"Tiny bubbles in my wine.
Makes me happy.
It makes me feel fine.
Tiny bubbles in my whiskey.
Makes me happy.
It makes me feel frisky."
"You get a line, I get a pole, honey, honey,
you get a line and I get a pole babe, babe.
You get a line, I get a pole,
we'll go down to the fishing hole,
honey, oh, baby mine."

Cadence after cadence spouts from my mouth until I begin to run out of breath and am out of the dense woods. From here, I have to hike a long ascent with several worrisome areas.

It feels warmer today compared to any other day I have been on trail. The sun is out, which affects the snowpack. It makes me think of possible wet snow avalanches. I take my time and be smart about my every move. Although difficult, I am able to follow my footprints from the day before making several sections quicker to hike. I know where to take my crampons off and put them on. I know how steep each section ahead will be.

When I make it to the final climb before Rock Pass, I find a boulder to sit on and breathe. I look towards the left of the boulder, and as though it has been perfectly placed, a rock with a fossilized leaf in it lays there. I pick it up and begin to examine it, bringing it close to my eyes. It is only partially fossilized. Half of the leaf is stamped in while the other hangs freely. It is a wonderful distraction from this next section I have been dreading all day. What lays ahead is steep and technical, making me wonder how much easier this would have been without snow. I snap a photo of the rock and place it back down the way I found it.

I work up the courage to continue and make this next climb. I drop to my hands and knees and begin to work my way up. I attempt to follow the same route I laid out the day before. I stab my ice axe into the snow, followed by kicking in my crampons for footing. It is slow going and nerve-racking. It's a long way down should I slip. I remind myself to have three points of contact at all times. When I finally reach the top, I use a great deal of strength to work my way up and over the crevasse. From there, I drop to the ground and roll over on my back trying to catch my breath and take in what I had just accomplished. Filled with joy for tackling this tough section and making it to the Monument the day before, I am excited to come across anyone heading Southbound, to share the good news that I had made it. I want to tell them how to get over and down Rock Pass. Just days before, I ran into several hikers, so my hopes are high. However, I come across zero hikers all day. Without phone service, I cannot even share my intel online that I have successfully crossed.

After a tenth of a mile from Rock Pass, the trail becomes snow-free for the next four miles. I can move a little quicker and enjoy the freedom from the cumbersome crampons or microspikes. This is until I reach a wooden sign telling me that Hart's Pass is fourteen miles ahead. From here, snow covers the trail again, but I only need to wear microspikes this time. Running streams flowing under the snow have overtaken the trail. There are a lot of sunken holes from hikers postholing into them. After postholing a few times myself, I soon end up hiking right along the trail, avoiding caving into it. My trekking poles come in handy, keeping me upright and balanced.

The day flies by, and the sun is starting to set. I have a mile left to hike. I make my way past Windy Pass and the area where my sister and cousin had turned back around a few days prior. I decide that after this small section, I will camp for the night. The temperature has already begun to drop. I don't want to waste time preparing a meal, so I will wait until I have made it to camp before eating. I am at mile twenty-five before I finally make it and am completely exhausted. It is late, and I am incredibly hungry and cold. I drop my pack, back covered in sweat. I open it as quickly as my cold fingers can move. I put on my dry long sleeve top, hoodie, a down jacket, and place a clean neck gaiter over my ears. I set my extra pair of dry, clean socks and Smartwool leggings atop my pack and will put them on once I am ready for bed. Aside from my hoodie, these are my sleep clothes only to be worn at night. I know that once my body starts to cool, I will shiver even more than when I am wearing wet clothing.

I grab my stove. I can barely feel my fingers now. I blow warm air onto them and proceed to connect my heater to the small can of propane I have been lugging around. This effort seems tedious as my fingers are slow to move. I pour water into my titanium mug and place it on the stove to boil. It is difficult to get my lighter started with my cold and frozen fingers. I look over at a small fire ring. Ahhh, a fire would be so nice right now. My clothes and shoes are soaked from having to crawl in the snow and cross streams these past days. I could dry them around a fire. I poorly attempt to grab some dry logs, but everything around me is soaking wet, and I soon give up. No fire tonight.

I reach back inside my pack, this time pulling out my tent. It only takes a few minutes to set up, and I toss my pack inside of it. I drop to my knees and reach back into my hiking pack. I pull out my bear bag. I grab a Ziplock freezer bag full of tonight's dinner, Oryx chili. It reminds me of my husband and brings a smile to my face. He has been deployed for just over a month now. I set my bear bag aside.

The water has come to a boil by then, so I pour it into my Ziplock bag. I get inside my tent. I am so cold. I then grab my sleeping pad and quilt, kick off my shoes, and pull off my wet socks. I get into my dry wool leggings, and pull my quilt over me. I place my dry socks into my quilt to warm them up to get them toasty right before I fall asleep. I really shouldn't be eating inside my tent because it can attract animals, such as mice, bears, mountain lions, and whatever else may be in search of food. I know all this but still don't exit my tent. My food and sleeping bag are so warm. I sit there trying to eat, teeth chattering as my body tries to warm up. I turn my inReach on and message my family letting them know I am safe and have made it to camp.

I climbed six passes today and only made it twenty-five miles. At this pace, how am I going to make it forty-two miles a day for the next two months? I am mentally beating myself up. I lower my head, start to doze off, food in hand, spork in mouth, completely exhausted. *No!* I shake my head to wake myself up. *You must eat. Food is fuel, and fuel is energy.* I try to devour everything quickly so I can curl up inside my quilt and sleep. But there is still one thing left to do. I don't bother putting my socks on; they are soaking wet anyway. I step each foot nimbly inside my cold, wet shoes. I slowly unzip my tent, teeth still chattering and fingers still cold. I crawl out. It is pitch black outside, so I reach for my headlamp. I walk toward the opposite side of the trail and away from camp. I spot a group of trees bunched together and tie my bear bag onto one of them. I go to the bathroom and walk as fast as I can back to my tent. Once I am warm and cozy inside, I grab all my electronics and place them inside my sleeping quilt. I use my powerbank to charge my watch and inReach. Amazingly, my watch has lasted three days and is still powered at thirty-eight percent. I hope to record the entire distance I am hiking on this thing. I grab my phone and look over the map for tomorrow's distance. I make a mental note of how far it is to Hart's Pass and set a goal of where I will camp the next day. Just thirty-five miles ahead.

Hopefully, the trail conditions will be better tomorrow. Within minutes, I am sound asleep. I am warm and cozy. It feels like I have only been asleep for minutes, but hours have actually passed when my alarm goes off.

CHAPTER 10

DAY 2 FKT ATTEMPT

July 5 - 7:50 a.m.

32.42 miles / 5,673 feet

13 hours, 51 minutes

"I'm knocked out. I've never felt so physically and mentally exhausted. I'm quite stupid with it and long only for bed, but I am happy."

-Claude Monet

I HEAR THE RINGING of my phone's alarm, but I ignore it while it continues to chime and buzz. I'm too cozy to reach over and turn it off. I mentally tell myself, *Get up!*

I take a deep breath and slowly exhale. Condensation comes from my mouth, making it look like I am blowing out a tiny cloud. How cold is it outside, anyway? I don't want to get out of my warm and cozy sleeping quilt. I grab my inReach and message my mom that I am getting ready to start hiking again. I reach for my cold, wet socks. My feet hurt, my legs hurt, everything hurts. I am so sore. *You just have to get moving and you will warm up*, I tell myself. I get up, slowly pull my leggings off, and crawl into my wet clothing. My pants are wet, my socks are wet, and my shoes are wet. Everything is cold, but I am finally dressed. I exit my tent when my inReach starts to chime. It is my mom sending me well wishes. Her message says she has asked the creator to have the eagles watch over me today. This fills my heart.

I grab my stove to boil water for my PERC Coffee and warm breakfast. I am moving at a snail's pace. I time myself. It takes me almost twenty minutes to pack up, a lot slower than I want. Tomorrow I need to be quicker. The clock keeps ticking no matter my pace, regardless of how fast or slow I move. The ongoing timer only stops when I press stop at the trail's finish line. I pack up my stove and eat my favorite breakfast, dehydrated biscuits and gravy on the go. The sun comes up and fills me with its warmth. I spend the morning admiring nature and giving gratitude towards everything I see.

I trek back to Hart's Pass excited to use the privy at the start of the trail. Privies seem like a slight upgrade compared to an outhouse or having to go in the woods. I soon learn just how few and far between these are. When I think about privies, I imagine the most gruesome and disgusting ones I have ever been inside. The kind where the floor is covered in pee and fecal matter runs across the seats. Where the smell is so unbearable and flies roam freely in and around while you're going. Spiders make their homes into the corners of the building, covering the walls with their webs. They make you hesitant to sit with the possibility of being bit. Sometimes there are even mice scampering about. Then you decide just to hold it no matter how badly you have to go. At this point, I don't care. I will take a smelly fly-infested privy any day just to sit on a regular toilet seat. If there are mounds of poo everywhere, I'll make a run for it.

I throw my pack off placing it on a huge boulder next to the privy. I reach up and rub my shoulders. My left one in particular unbearably aches today. I move my head from side to side and in circular motions in an attempt to stretch my neck out. I take a deep breath like it is the start of a race, before going for it. I enter the privy, and to my surprise, it doesn't smell. In fact, I don't smell any odors or see a single fly. No fecal matter on the seat or pee on the ground appears. The privy is spotless, and it is well stocked with toilet paper. This is the most immaculate privy I have ever seen. There is even a garbage can inside, perfect for getting rid of all my empty food wrappers. I want to applaud whoever takes care of this privy.

When I am done using the restroom and put my pack back on, I grimace at the pain of tightening my hip belt. Trying to take most of the weight off my shoulders, I cinch it just a little tighter than normal. I tighten my right shoulder strap to take the weight off of my left shoulder. This provides just a small amount of relief but is far more uncomfortable overall. I soon adjust everything back to the way it was.

Once I have set off and am well past the privy, I am met with a field full of dead trees. Just two years prior, the Diamond Creek Fire devastated the area, burning over 100,000 acres. It reached this part of the trail and is the first burned field I have seen. There are downed and burned trees still upright everywhere. It is not a place anyone would or should camp. New growth is beginning to take place, though, with the abundance of bright, green grass everywhere.

It is another five miles before I make it to Glacier Pass. The sun shines bright and with every step I take, its warmth slowly dries my clothes. It does very little for my wet and soggy soles, though. I pass a few day hikers and find myself alongside another snow-covered mountain. I try not to let frustration get the best of me as I am forced to put on crampons. These thoughts are soon forgotten as I am halted once again. Only this time it is a loud but prevalent noise. I look up and see two beautiful bald eagles soaring atop of me. Their loud, high-pitched, whistling calls bring happy tears and a smile to my face, reminding me of my mother's message this morning. I pull out my phone and begin to video them. I want to show her. I want to show my kids and my husband the beauty of this place and of these creatures. I want to share this experience with them.

It took me three days to reach the Monument, and I am currently on day two of my Southbound FKT. As I continue to hike, my wet socks begin taking a toll on my feet. I have spent almost five days hiking in soaking wet socks and shoes. Although the sun has dried my clothes, walking through the snow has kept my feet constantly wet. I am wearing trail shoes and have nothing to protect my heels from the straps of the crampons. Even with tall socks, blisters start to form on my heels, and I have deep blisters forming on both sides of my big toes. I do my best to protect them from further damage. I reach into my pack and pull out my first aid kit. It contains several bandages, a small roll of medical tape, a needle and thread, bacitracin, and a long strip of rolled-up duct tape. For medicine, I have Tylenol and some anti-nausea pills. After I have what I need, I begin to lather my feet up with Trail Toes cream followed by placing bandages over them. This helps alleviate most of the pain and will hopefully prevent further blistering.

Once I cover another ten miles across snow to Methow Pass, I am surprised by the view of the mountain in front of me. There is a small lake just below, and a nice 500-foot descent without snow. Another bird soars above me, and I take out my phone to capture it on video. Thinking it is another bald eagle, I am soon proven wrong. It soars above me, as if telling me, "I am not an eagle, but a hawk." Another reminder of my mom's message.

This section is beyond magical, full of flowing streams and carpets of green. I stop to quickly filter water for the sixth time today. With the amount of water available along the trail, I only need to fill up one to two bottles at a time. This helps lighten my pack and prevents long water carries.

I pull out my lunch for the day: two large tortillas with two packets of hazelnut spread. I hike and eat, doing my best to take my time and savor every bite. I even open the packets and lick the remaining hazelnut spread until there is nothing left.

The evening appears quickly and after traversing more snow today, I decide to end the night at mile marker 57.7, just a few miles shy of today's goal. By ten in the evening, I am ready for bed. But I spend the night tossing and turning, fallout from the weight of my pack and long hours on my feet. I am achy, and my stomach begins to throw a tantrum. It did not agree with this evening's dinner of tostadas and beans. I end up waking up several times throughout the night to use the restroom.

CHAPTER 11

DAY 3 FKT ATTEMPT

July 6 - 7:09 a.m.

38.52 miles / 4,800 feet

14 hours, 49 minutes

"There are wounds that never show on the body that are deeper and more hurtful than anything that bleeds."

-Laurel K. Hamilton

ANOTHER SLOW START TO MY MORNING. Yesterday's 5,000-foot descent really took a toll on my legs. I work to stretch them out and massage my quadriceps. I take another look at my map and the location I had picked out last night for today. I try ignoring my negative thoughts of trailing behind the schedule. To keep positive, I find something to get excited about and focus on making it to the North Cascades National Park.

I am faced with so many different types of bridges and water crossings today. Some bridges have railings, while others don't. Some bridges are made up of just a single log. Some crossings have big boulders you step on to make your way across. Other crossings offer little support, forcing you to walk through the water to the other side. At mile 71.1, I hike across one of the coolest bridges I have seen since starting the PCT. It is unlike any others. There are no logs helping to ease my way across. Instead, this bridge is only held up by cables making for a wobbly crossing. I keep my balance by grabbing the two cables that are chest height. A waterfall runs below, clearly seen through open slats of wood making up the crossing. Knowing no one is around, I yell, "This is so cool!"

Once I make it to the National Park, I realize this trail section is a bit different than what I have been trekking across all week. The trail is lush, surrounded by miles of bright green terrain. Unlike the trail before the North Cascades National Park, this portion is free and clear of downed trees and snow. A much-needed relief.

Having hiked days in snowy and cold conditions, my body retaliates at the warmth of lower altitude. I roll up my long sleeve shirt and pants. My face feels warm, and I feel a rush of fluid beginning to flow down my nose. I reach up to touch my nostril. I take one look at my finger and see blood. I try to react as quickly as possible without getting any blood on my clothes. I reach for my tissue placed in the front pouch of my waist belt. I ball the tissue together and stuff it into my nostril. I continue hiking and pull out the tissue once the bleeding has stopped.

The rest of the trail is clearly marked and full of small rolling hills. I pick up my pace today, which has made my feet hurt earlier than normal. I find a small stream to sit at and remove my shoes and socks. I walk barefoot to the middle, where a rock is peeking out above the water, and take a seat. With my feet submerged, the cold flowing water makes them ache a little more until they grow used to the temperature.

I take off my shirt and socks, dunking them into the water until the grime and dirt have washed away. A bath would be nice, but the water is too cold to submerge fully. Making sure no one is around, I scoop up handfuls of water and begin to clean the rest of my body.

When I am finished cleaning up, I return back to my backpack. I hang my socks from the D-ring on my pack and put my dry sleep socks on. My pants feel baggy today. No matter how much I try to tighten them, they continue to sag. They have started to become an annoyance, and it's time to finally do something about it. I look over at my socks and then at the one D-ring I have securing them. I remove my socks and the D-ring. The D-ring isn't very big, and I am able to weave it through my front two pant loops. This seems to do the trick, as my pants remain above my hips. I take my socks and place them over my tent poles on the outside of my pack.

It doesn't take me long to reach the High Bridge Historical Cabin in the Park. I really want to check it out, but there is already another female hiker up ahead talking with a Ranger. Keeping within social distance guidelines, I forgo the idea and hike on.

It is getting late, and I have five miles left to go before reaching my predetermined camp site. I try to hike just a little bit faster, but I am overheated from the rise in today's temperature. The change of weather causes another rush of blood to flow from my nose. I quickly lean forward, letting it drip onto the ground in front of me. I reach for my tissue once again and stuff a piece of it into my nostril. The tissue quickly fills with blood. I pull it out and stuff another one back in place. My other nostril begins to emit the same amount of fluid. I now have tissues stuffed into both nostrils. I think to myself, *I don't have time for this*. I need to keep going because I am running out of daylight. While walking, I pinch the top part of my nose and tilt my head slightly back to stop the bleeding. Minutes pass, and still no improvement. Every tissue I ball up into my nose gets filled with blood instantly. I finally stop to wait until the bleeding has subsided. I tilt my head back even further. The warm blood rushes to the back of my throat and into my mouth. It tastes disgusting, and I start to spit it out. With my head tilted back, I pour cool water onto my face and neck. My body is overheated. Blood continues to enter the back of my throat and into my mouth.

The smell and taste of warm blood reminds me of treating a casualty during deployment. I was working an overnight shift at the hospital. This was a time before the medics in our company were assigned to convoys. I remember standing there, watching as four soldiers carried a local Iraqi towards us. He was on a litter, lying on his stomach, with his head on a blood-soaked pillow. The blood dripped onto the floor as they set his litter down. Even before we started working to save his life, we knew the end result. I could see it in everyone's eyes. He was too far gone, and his wounds were severe. At the time, Tim was a pharmacy technician. We weren't married or even a couple yet. He had also been called in to help deliver the drugs. I wondered

if he could smell the blood, too. To this day, I have nev
him about it. As the doctor and nurse worked their magic and
directed us on what to do, I glanced at the crimson pillow, trying to figure out what the original color was. Every inch of it
was blood-soaked, and it continued dripping with blood. There
was so much blood, and the smell was so strong I could taste it.

Thinking of this as the blood flows towards the back of my
throat and into my mouth causes me to gag. The gagging soon
turns into vomiting, taking my dinner and its precious calories
with it. I have never had a bloody nose this bad before. I haven't
even thought much about the Iraqi we treated until now. When
my nose finally decides to stop bleeding, I can feel clots of blood
stuck in each nostril. I leave the clots in place, worried that if I
try to blow them out, my nose will start bleeding again. I grab
my toothbrush from my hip belt pocket and begin to brush
away the disgusting taste of vomit and blood. I brush my teeth
over and over again until the taste vanishes.

Am I suffering? I think to myself. *Will I continue to have flashbacks throughout my hike? Will this get any better? Will I feel any
better?* When I run ultramarathons, I have always found that the
suffering doesn't ever go away, I just begin to build a tolerance.
Will I feel the same throughout my hike?

When I finally make it to camp, the noise of the nearby creek
is a welcoming sound and distraction from how my evening has
unraveled so far. It is the perfect location for filtering my water
in the morning. The area near the creek is also a large established campsite big enough to fit at least five tents. Once again, I
am the only one around and have the entire place to myself. I

look at my map for tomorrow. I have made it to mile marker 93.1, even though my watch says I should have traveled much further. I am guessing backtracking has added the extra mileage. Either way, I am excited to get my first 100 miles out of the way tomorrow.

CHAPTER 12

July 7 - 7:54 a.m.

29.82 miles / 7,382 feet

13 hours, 41 minutes

"Without the anticipation of better things ahead, we will have no heart for the journey."

-John Eldredge

I SLEEP IN UNTIL 7:20 A.M. The cold mornings continue to make getting out of my warm quilt difficult. I am incredibly sore and stiff. It takes my body time to get warmed up and going. With the scarce amount of food I have left, I am worried that I will run out of food before reaching my first resupply point. I also only have one battery pack remaining. As I begin to lay out my food for the day, I know I have enough for about four days. Even with the extra snacks I packed, I did not calculate the extra time it would take me to reach my first resupply point. Trekking through snow has greatly slowed my progress.

If I am going to make it, I need to devise a plan. I need to spread out what calories I have left. I set aside 1,200 calories for the day, which is not even a third of the calories I should be consuming each day. I gained an extra ten pounds going into the start of this hike and feel as though I have already lost it all and much more.

For breakfast, I have another cup of PERC Coffee but limit my food intake to one packet of apple cinnamon oatmeal. For lunch, I will eat one packet of lemon pepper tuna with some peanut butter crackers. I will snack on another packet of peanut butter crackers and jerky for the day. I also set aside three small pieces of Laffy Taffy, one of my favorite candies. I will cut my dinner in half. Eat half tonight and the other half tomorrow. It all sounds terrible, and a part of me just wants to tear open all my food and eat everything in one sitting.

Today's hike starts with a 2,500-foot climb within the first seven miles. From there, the trail drops almost 4,000 feet in ten miles and then back to a climb. After hiking a few miles, I come to a fast-flowing stream. I search for a safer route. I hike a little ways down only to find that the water flow speeds up and rapids form. I decide to return back to where I left the trail and try my hand at walking across the water, avoiding the faster-flowing portions. With each step, the stream's icy cold flow courses around my legs, reaching just below my waist. The coldness actually feels good on my tired and sore legs, making each step feel rejuvenating. When I finally make it to the other side, I squeeze as much water from my pants as possible. I remove my socks and drain the water from them as well, and then repeat the process with my insoles. Moving forward, the snow returns, and the trail becomes lost once again.

After hiking for a few minutes, I get excited to see another hiker behind me. I secretly hope that she will catch up and pass me so that I can follow her tracks. Within the first mile of seeing her, she vanishes. She probably turned back around.

I continue on, Guthook app in hand. The trail is really difficult to follow. Footprints are sporadic, with some leading the wrong direction. Some of the trees are half buried, which make me nervous to cross them. Adding to my nervousness, one tree manages to free itself and whack me in the face. I fall back onto my bottom and my water filter flask slips from my front pack pocket. It slides down ten feet before coming to a halt. A part of me just wants to leave it and not put forth the effort to retrieve it. I know I need it, though. I use the tree to support my pack and pull out my ice axe. I slowly work my way down to my filter, retrieve it, and then return to my pack. When placing my flask back, I make sure to secure it with the band of the pouch.

When I make it to the top of Cloudy Pass, around mile marker 100, I enjoy my long descent. The snow begins to vanish the further down I hike, and I pick up my pace and jog a good portion of trail. I pass two female hikers taking a nap next to the trail near a tree. The tree is so big it covers two portions of the trail. We briefly greet one another as I make my way past them.

I see that the trail maintenance crew did an excellent job clearing this section. No shrubs or dead trees overtake the trail. Even the tree lying on the ground in front of me has been taken care of by them. Usually, the trail maintenance crew will remove whatever trees have fallen on the trail, but this one is simply too massive. Instead, the crew left the tree where it fell and sawed out a chunk of wood from it to allow hikers the proper footing for climbing over. Once I am past it, I begin jogging again until I turn and reach the other half of this downed tree. Again, I can't believe how massive this tree is to take up several sections of the trail during these switchbacks.

When I am up and over again, I continue my jog. A few more downed trees on the trail slow my progress, but I make up some lost time by continuing to jog. I continue at this pace until I reach the base and begin a steady climb up towards the next pass.

The trail soon passes alongside a waterfall. At the fall's base, the water runs rampant exactly where the trail crosses. This stream is seasonal, but deciding to hike early means the snow melt is causing a strong flow. This fast-flowing water makes me hesitant to cross. If I slip and fall, it will be a long and rocky fall into rushing water. Everything in my gut tells me to stop to find another way. There has to be another way. I step off the trail and follow the stream further down. The water's flow grows stronger here. There are several downed trees that may make it possible to cross. Some trees have broken off into the stream, while others lay alongside it. After a tenth of a mile spent searching, I spot a downed tree laying perfectly upright from one side of the stream to the next. I slowly make my way towards it, weaving around and between trees in the process. I take a seat and begin to scoot my way across. The tree is so thin that it reminds me of basic training, where we had to traverse from one side of a rope to the next. Only here, there is no safety net, and no one will be around to rescue me if I should fall.

My feet dangle on each side of the tree as water rushes rapidly beneath them. But the tree is at an upright angle and too skinny for comfort. After a few forward scoots and almost losing balance, I decide not to go any further and slowly scoot my way back and off of the tree. I hike another fifty feet up, and there I see it. A huge log next to two other smaller logs hovering over the water. It is covered in moss and just wide enough to allow me safe passage. I quickly make my way towards it, drop to my hands and knees, and slowly crawl my way across. The water continues to flow heavily just underneath. Within minutes I reach the other side safely. I let out a huge sigh of relief and take a giant swig of water. I hike back up to where I left the trail only on the opposite side of the stream. I can't believe how much time and effort it took just to make it to this side of the trail. A mere ten feet from the other side. Yet again, everything that seems so simple and sounds easy on paper hasn't been.

I hike on through the cold and drizzly rain until I come to an intersection. Today has been gloomy. The evening sky is overcast, making it impossible for my Guthook guide to work effectively. The sunlight fades quickly. I hope I am going the right way. I soon pass a PCT emblem relieving me of all my anxiety. At least I can follow the trail down here, and I have been fortunate enough to spend most of the day without snow.

The woods give off an eerie feeling. Not a single chirp can be heard nor the sound of chipmunks and squirrels scurrying in the distance. It is quiet. Almost too quiet, and for the first time since I have started my trek, I feel completely alone. *Is there a storm coming? Why is it so quiet?* I continue on, talking to myself.

My mind starts to stray towards Iraq and my first encounter with an explosive device. It was my first mission out, and I was nervous. Our convoy was in charge of escorting semi-trucks to another base. Everything seemed so surreal at the time. I was only twenty-two years old and didn't know how much this deployment would change me. An EFP (explosively formed penetrator) flew from one side of the road to the other during that mission. Only it made contact with the truck in front of us. As we watched what just happened through the front window of our humvee, the convoy leader turned to me and said, "Doc, get your aid bag ready."

I remember trying to calm my nerves, thinking, *This can't be real. I am not ready for this.* I took a few deep breaths and said a prayer, hoping that the man inside the semi-truck was okay, and if he was hurt, he only had minor injuries. As we drove near his vehicle, the driver jumped out. We all looked at each other in shock that he was still alive. The EFP had flown directly through his side window and exited through the roof of his vehicle, barely missing him. Before we could leave the area, it was protocol to wait for the semi-truck to burn to the ground. As we sat there watching the truck go up in flames, I remember thinking how lucky the man was and how lucky we were. If the EFP had gone off a few seconds later, it could have hit us, and I may not be here today. It's surprising how the trail can bring up experiences I have worked so hard to ignore. I'm lost in thought when the rain drops, which have grown in size, smack me back to reality.

I struggle to shift my thoughts back to the trail by focusing on other things, like calculating the miles I need to hike per day to finish within my permitted time frame. I begin a steady, dark climb with a few switchbacks. It is seven-thirty, and I need to make it to camp by nine.

I stop and hunker down under a tree using it's long, thick branches to help block the rain. I pull my rain pants on and take out my stove. I need a warm dinner. My hands are cold, and my gloves are soaked. I boil water and add it to my dehydrated meal of Mexican rice and beans. I place the bag between my hands, warming them. Since I am only eating half a meal, I make it extra watery, turning it into a nice, hot soup. It should be enough to fill me up and keep my stomach from growling for the rest of the evening. I quickly pack my stove and continue hiking, eating along the way. With over 1,000 feet of climbing left before I make it to camp, I'm determined to make it, even though I have already climbed over 6,000 feet today. The trail has turned to mud, and I know I will be hitting snow again soon.

Just then, something catches my eye, and I hike closer to exam it. At my feet and centered on the trail is a huge hawk feather. It is perfectly shaped, clean of mud or grime, and shimmers slightly. I hear my great grandfather Albert Madplume's voice in the back of my head telling me he intentionally dropped this feather for me. My aunt told me that in our Blackfeet culture, my great grandfather takes on the form of a hawk. Could the hawk feather be a gift from him?

Besides a few greetings from hikers here and there, the passing days have remained mostly isolated, and I haven't had a real conversation with anyone. Maybe my great grandfather's voice are whispers inside my manic mind. Realizing I may be going crazy, I step over the feather to continue hiking. But something in my mind tells me to stop and go back until I have retrieved the feather. I follow my intuition and pick up the feather stuffing it into my pack's mesh.

I am grateful and make an offering as a thank you. I grab two spoonfuls of my dinner, placing the food on a boulder next to me. I thank my great grandfather for this gift and ask that he continues to watch over me. It just feels like the right thing to do, and for the first time today, I feel that I am not alone. I continue to hike on.

As I turn towards the next switchback, I meet a deer standing directly in front of me. It looks at me in wonder, as if it is thinking, *What are you doing way up here?* Maybe this creature has never seen a human. I start walking towards it thinking it will run off, but instead, it stays standing. Unbothered by my forward motion, it continues standing and staring in my direction. I click my trekking poles together and tell the deer to excuse me. As though it understands, it slowly walks further up the mountain and off the trail, continuing to gaze in my direction. As I pass, it loses interest and continues back to what it had been doing before I arrived: eating.

Gray clouds blanket the sky and the sunlight turns pitch black. I reach snow once again. I attempt to follow the footsteps of the brave hikers who forged this trail days or possibly weeks before me. With my Guthooks app not cooperating today, I decide that once I reach the next designated camping area, I will call it quits for the night. Besides, it has begun pouring rain, and I can't wait to take shelter.

I approach camp by nine-thirty and set up at Dolly Vista, mile 121.1, 5,739 feet above sea level. It is the only section I have come across in the past hour not completely covered in snow. Tall trees surround one side of it, blocking most of the rain. When hanging my bear bag, I cover it with my poncho, hoping to help keep my bag dry. The temperature has dropped significantly since sunset. I stay as warm as possible by moving quickly and changing into my sleep clothes.

Once settled in, I try to save my inReach battery life and press the automated message button on my SPOT device. I've created the message before my hike, and it is set to message my brother, sister, mother, and husband. The premade message reads, "I have made it to camp, or I am just leaving camp, but am safe." It cannot receive messages, but SPOT can send a preset one.

I wake shivering in the middle of the night, the frigid temperatures chilling me to the bone.

CHAPTER 13

DAY 5 FKT ATTEMPT

July 8 - 6:37 a.m.

19.73 miles / 5,531 feet

16 hours, 16 minutes

"Together we took the paths that run
west of moon and east of sun."

-Dark Warriors Cache,
1966-1980, My Great Hart

MY BLADDER WAKES ME UP at five, well before my alarm goes off. I lay in bed for thirty minutes battling to fall back asleep. I know it's freezing out. Last night was the coldest night I have experienced since the start of the trail. I am glad I have layers of warm clothing to keep me from freezing at night. I try to go back to sleep and stay cuddled up inside my cozy quilt but soon lose the fight. I need to go to the bathroom badly and cannot hold it any longer. I jump out of bed and wobble away from camp towards my bear bag. I return minutes later, bag in hand, not bothering to get back in bed. I am not close to any nearby streams, so I grab a chunk of snow and place it into my stove to boil. I eat half a bag of biscuits and gravy for breakfast and wash it down with a cup of coffee.

I decide to eat breakfast at the campsite, watching the sunrise. The mountain ranges off in the distance are beyond gorgeous. Partially covered in snow, their peaks are visible as the clouds float just below them. I mentally check off two bucket list items: "Sit and watch the sunrise" and "Be above the clouds."

As I sit in this peaceful spot, I begin to prepare my mind for today. Because I am so high up, I know I will spend most of my day in the snow. Just as I am finishing my breakfast, a deer peeks out from the woods and greets me. She steadily walks into camp, feeding off the land in front of me. Just like the deer yesterday, this one is not threatened by my presence. She looks majestic above the clouds, grazing away as the sun is rising in the background. She gradually works her way down the mountain and into the tree line. I don't move from my spot until she is out of sight.

Once she is gone, I finally get up and start moving. I finish loading my hiking pack with all my gear and cover my shoes with the dreaded crampons. I take one last look at the mountain range behind me and begin to hike my way up and over this mountain.

I pause several times to check if the map on my phone is sending me in the right direction. The mountain varies from steep to less steep, and I use the tree line and dry patches of land to help ease my way across. I carefully make my way up and over the mountain. The sun rises on top of me and shines brightly on this side of the mountain. As I begin my descent, a red placard catches my eye. It is pinned to a tree with a quote, "Together we took the paths that run west of moon and east of sun, Dark Warriors Cache, 1966-1980, My Great Hart." What does this quote mean?

Thankful for a warm, sunlit, and snowless side, I remove my crampons, thinking about the quote, trying to put it into my own words. *There will come a day when our time on earth has come to an end.* Perhaps it is a memorial commemorating life. *But, just like the sun rises and falls, so do people.*

I put the quote behind me, thankful the following seven miles are full of switchbacks with barely any snow. I bushwhack my way down as efficiently as possible, but before long, my left foot catches a hidden root. I tumble forward, falling on my hips and stomach. *OUCH!* I am slow to get up. Besides some new bruises, the fall did not cause any injuries, so I keep going. Moments later, my left foot catches something again. I stumble forward but catch my balance and manage to avoid a fall. I look back to see what caused me to trip. This time, I spot a sharp rock sticking halfway out of the ground. *Just slow down,* I tell myself. I am not too fond of this section.

Bears love this type of terrain, and I don't want to see any of them. I begin to hum and talk to myself as the bushes become denser. When I grow tired of talking, I tap my trekking poles together now and then until I reach the bottom.

The trail eventually crosses over a large footbridge placed over Milk Creek. The running water flows from Glacier Peak's Ptarmigan Glacier. The stream is strong and mesmerizing. Once

I have made it across the bridge, I sit down to admire its intense beauty. I take a few nibbles of my lunch and look up at my next obstacle. What goes down must go up. Only this part rises 2,000 feet in three miles. I climb just as slowly as my descent and meet with patches of snow over and over again. The giant mounds of snow lay directly on the trail with no other way around but up and over.

After climbing 1,000 feet, the snowless land disappears, and I confront trekking through the white-covered trail. I am optimistic and hope that once I reach the top, the snow will be minimal on the other side. My optimism soon fades when I see the snow-capped top, but I still need to make my way over Firecreek Pass. I can hear running water beneath the snow, and I take my time following the trail in step with my phone's directions as closely as possible. If I go the wrong way, it could mean a plunge into this freezing stream.

The sun beats down on my face as I slowly make my way up towards the Pass. I see the footsteps of the hikers who braved the trail before me. I spot a break in the snow where the water runs through, a signal that someone may have stepped into the icy water. I dare not follow their route, so I take a few more steps further up from theirs. I jab my trekking pole into the snow in front of me as hard as possible, trying to determine if it is safe to step forward. I continue to do this until I reach the stream where I must pass. The water is flowing fast. I look up and down the snowbank searching for an easy place to jump across. Everything looks the same. I don't want to risk stepping anywhere else. I know I can make this. *You got this*, I say to myself. I make a giant leap over the stream and successfully land on the other side. My heart beats fast, and I slowly continue climbing while trying to catch my breath simultaneously.

Finally, I scramble over this portion of the mountain, and right away, something baby blue catches my eye. It is a lake surrounded by snow. The lake's reflection is so strong that it looks like the sky was placed on the ground with white fluffy clouds surrounding it. The soft colors bring my heartbeat down to a steady pace. I can sit here for hours gazing into the lake's icy cold-core. It is so quiet and peaceful up here. As if this moment in time mirrors the lake, both frozen and still. I take a few deep breaths and close my eyes. I want to remember this feeling and the beauty of this place forever. I grab my phone from my coat pocket to take a picture. Although the photo turns out beautifully, it does not capture the stunning majesty of this place. Photos seldomly do.

I look at the map on my phone once again, making sure I am on the correct path. I notice the trail curves, so I point it toward the direction I will eventually go. Suddenly, I feel my heartbeat pulsating in the back of my throat. *Oh no! That cannot be the correct way.* I look at my phone once again and take a big gulp as if trying to change the direction of the trail magically. But no luck. Nothing changes. I look off in the distance toward the opposite side of where the trail leads and the sun hits. The snow is minimal there and seems like an easier option. *Why can't the trail go that way? That mountain looks easier to climb. Why can't this just get easier?* I can't fixate on these thoughts. I place my phone back into my pocket and continue moving forward.

The next tenth of a mile is wide, not too steep, and allows me time to relax. The rest is short-lived, though, as I approach a vertical section on the side of the mountain. I take my time crossing, and this is where things go wrong.

People who've experienced near-death encounters will often say that right before your imminent death, life flashes before your eyes. The saying stood true for me at this moment. Time sped up, and then everything happened within a blink of an eye. And in those moments, my thoughts shifted toward survival. *This can't be it; this can't be the end.* I attempt to stab my ice axe into the snow, and my foot slips out in front of me. I start to fall. My trekking pole slips from my grasp. I try to stab my ice axe into the snow once more but miss. I start sliding toward the base of this mountain. I try to jab my ice axe into the snow again, this time making contact, but momentum picks up speed, and the axe slips from my hand and narrowly out of my reach. I start punching my hands into the snow, but nothing happens. I continue sliding. I can't grab anything to stop. All that lies ahead and below is just snow.

Please don't panic, I think to myself. If I kick my crampons into the snow, I can break an ankle, but it's all I've got left. Luckily, the mountain's steepness starts to mellow out, giving me a little time to kick my heel in, and it works. I stop suddenly. Adrenaline pumping, I turn my body toward the mountain and kneel. I take a step and slip again but fall into the mountain, preventing a plunge further down.

Still kneeling, I throw my pack off and grab my other trekking pole from the mesh. It's a steep climb up, and without my trekking pole, it would almost be impossible. As I ascend, I kick each foot into the snow two times before stepping. This pattern provides a better footing for each step. Kick, kick, step with one foot, kick, kick, step with the other foot. I follow each step with a jab of my trekking pole into the snow. I make the point to stay low. If I slip again, I can punch my knees forward toward the mountain.

I take off my gloves for better grip and make sure my grasp is firm on the trekking pole. I use the pole to pull myself up. I slowly climb my way to where my ice axe and trekking pole stand, exactly where I left them. I first reach my ice axe and pull it out of the snow. I make sure to wrap the strap tightly around my wrist, so I don't risk the chance of it slipping away from me if I fall again. With a trekking pole in one hand and an ice axe in the other, I continue climbing up, heading towards the other trekking pole. I pull the second trekking pole out, kick a hole into the snow, and sit. I look down toward where I slid. That must be thirty feet at least. Breathing heavily, I sit there for a few minutes and realize this has been the sketchiest section yet, and now I am scared.

I message my husband. "Stopped to sit for a breather. This is way beyond my comfort zone. I don't know, honey." Maybe he will get this message, but perhaps he won't. I am too afraid to tell him what just happened. I only need encouragement, so it's worth a shot. He does not respond. Still deployed, and because of the significant time difference, he will not get my message until later in the evening. I message my mom. I want to message her that I am scared and tell her what I am about to do and what just happened, but I don't. I don't want to worry her. Another flashback enters my mind. Whenever I called her from Iraq, I would always tell her I was safe, working in some hospital. In reality, I was going out on dangerous convoy missions. I am just glad I don't have to lie to her over the phone now because it is much easier through text.

I keep it simple: "Hello mom, how are you?"

Her response comes ten minutes later. "Are you okay?"

Am I okay? I think to myself. *Can I climb this? Should I even try?* I doubt it can be any worse than if I turn back.

I stop again to rest and to think things through. This section of the trail is way beyond my comfort zone. I have already fallen, and my self-arrest of preventing myself from sliding further down the mountain was far from great. I don't know if I can do this. This is the first time I have questioned myself since the start of my hike. The first time I have been this afraid. The first time I have questioned my ability. The first time I felt as though I could actually fail and could severely injure myself. I doubt anyone would be able to reach me if I had to push my SOS button. I haven't seen anyone since yesterday. What if I fell into a crevasse or worse? What if I die? I wouldn't be found for weeks, months, or possibly ever. My heart beats faster. I take several deep breaths trying to calm my nerves.

I respond back to my mom. "This next section seems difficult." I am still trekking forward on the side of the snow-covered mountain, the pointy ice axe in one hand and my aluminum trekking pole in the other. *Slow is smooth, smooth is fast,* crosses my mind. *Don't rush things, take your time, be aware of your surroundings. Slow is smooth, smooth is fast,* I tell myself again and again.

My Garmin inReach chimes ten minutes later. It is my mother, "Be careful, Jess. Sounds challenging. Your Auntie Minnie said to ask your great-grandpa Albert Madplume to watch over you. His Indian name is Black Owl - Sic Sa Pis Du. I am praying for you. I love you." There is a large rock a few feet ahead, so I take a few steps towards it and sit again. I dig my heavy crampons into the snow. They rub against the top of my blistered ankles, but my heart beats too fast to feel the pain. I rest my pack on the rock and look back up at the mountain. I let her words sink in and start to pray.

I say my Indian name aloud: "Isht' PuTaki." Repeating my name gives me strength and courage. I pray that my ancestors continue to watch over me and guide me on the correct path. I thank my mother for her words of encouragement and wisdom. I thank the creator for keeping me safe thus far. If only my mother knew how much I needed these words at this moment. If only she knew what I was about to attempt or what I have been through so far. I take a deep breath. I think about my kids and husband and contemplate my next move.

My brother's voice echoes in my head. "Just take your time, sis. Look around and do not rush. Don't be afraid to turn back if you have to." It is something he whispered into my ear as he was hugging me goodbye from Windy Pass.

As I sit there thinking through his words, I search for a route up, but no trail appears and the footsteps I followed earlier are lost in the snow. I pull out jerky and munch on it. I take another look at the mountain and think again about how I will climb it. Then I spot something off in the distance. It's a marmot running up the mountain in the same direction I must go. He is moving from side to side as if he is floating his way to the top. He makes it look effortless. He is showing me the way. The shortest route would be to go straight up, but his side-to-side movements up show me this is the safest option. I stuff my jerky wrapper into my Ziploc bag and head toward the marmot's footsteps, slowly working my way up in the same direction as the animals. I dig my ice axe into the snow, followed by my trekking pole. I kick my crampons in for footing and progress toward my next obstacle. Stab, stab, and step, stab, stab, and step. It takes some effort and finesse, but I make it past.

I keep going, wishing my husband would respond. I face the next obstacle, the peak. There is a huge chunk of snow hanging from the top, and I need to somehow make my way over it without it falling and taking me down with it. I can see footprints in the snow once again, so I follow them. They guide me toward the ridge. This drop-off I had been staring at an hour ago shook me to my core just by looking at it. I don't know what lies beyond this Pass, but I know that there is no turning back once I cross over. I decide to take my chances and push on. Perhaps there will be less snow on the other side. Maybe I can finally ditch my crampons and ice axe. This thought continues to cross my mind with each pass I encounter.

While making my way over the ridge, I am on my knees, digging my crampons into the snow. To get a better grip, I am still not wearing gloves. I stab my ice axe in the snow, followed by my trekking pole, and stay as low as possible. If I slip, the fall follows a long way down, and at the bottom sits a frozen lake. Minutes pass like hours while sweat drips down my face. I continue on; stab, stab, and step. As I finally make it over, an immense wave of emotion rushes over me. I lay in the snow, exhausted, trying to catch my breath. I cannot believe I just did that. I found a certain strength I never knew I had. I thank the creator that I am safe. I thank my ancestors for guiding me and protecting me. I thank the marmot for showing me the way. For the first time since starting my hike, I don't hold anything back and let the tears flow.

When I finally sit back up, I wipe my face off and let out an enormous breath of air. I feel on top of the world. At this moment, I own the place all to myself and this view makes up for all the obstacles I've encountered so far.

I look off into the distance, searching for any sign of the trail. *Ugh*, more snow and no sign of tracks. I try not to take the snow and cold for granted because I know that the climate will completely transform once I reach California. Yet, I am ready to see the end of the snow and hope these trying days will pass quickly. Once I finish these sections, I can get rid of all this extra hiking gear.

As I begin the few steps forward, a loud noise stops me. It sounds like rocks falling in the distance. Maybe it's an avalanche. I see nothing unusual on this side of the mountain. The mysterious sound definitely starts from the other side. *Please don't let whatever is happening there happen anywhere near me.* The sounds disappear for a moment only to begin again after a few steps. Two jets fly over, followed by their thunderous roars, and just like that, they are gone. I'm hoping the jet noise does not cause an avalanche on this side of the mountain.

Despite the snow, I tell myself this part is much easier than if I had turned back. I break away from my thoughts, interrupted by a loud whistle. I yell, "HELLO!" No response. I keep hiking. I hear another whistle. I again scream, "HELLO! Is anyone there? Are you okay?" Haunted by flashbacks from my Army medic days, the whistle and jet engines summon the worst-case scenarios in my mind. Maybe the footprints I have been following mean someone is injured. I stop and listen again. I look around, trying to find the source and location of the sound. The whistle goes off again, and then I finally find it. *Are you kidding me?* I think to myself and begin to laugh. I cannot believe what I was thinking. It's not a person calling for help. No one needs medical attention. Instead, the biggest marmot I have ever seen in my life, resembling a huge beaver, looks at me and whistles again. I pick up my pace and start working my way towards it. The trail leads alongside its home, and it soon disappears into a hole in the ground. Another two jets, possibly the same ones, pass above me. I know they cannot see me, but I look up and wave anyway.

Since it is getting late, I decide on a new camp location just a few miles away for the night. My stomach grumbles in disagreement since I decided to wait until camp before eating dinner. My hunger begs me to stop here. But I am stubborn, and after how much snow I had to traverse today, I vow not to spend the night camped on it. I continue until eleven, when I finally reach an area free of snow. I am hungry and tired.

Unlike trail running, there is no one to hold your hand at the end of the day or aid station buffets to replenish lost calories. No rest stops wait for you, and no hot showers will warm you up. On the PCT, everything relies on you, no matter how tired you feel. Only you make dinner and set up camp. Only you warm yourself up.

It takes me forever to set up my tent. When I finish, I sit inside it replenishing today's lost calories. After dinner, I don't want to do anything but sit. I don't want to move a muscle and am annoyed at the fact I still have to hang my bear bag. I am glad I do because when I return to my tent, the shadow of a mouse catches my eye. The mouse continues to scurry around my tent even though I yell at it to go away. It begins to rain, causing the mouse to scamper off. As though listening to a lullaby, the musical sound of the rain pitter-pattering on my tent puts me to sleep.

CHAPTER 14

DAY 6 FKT ATTEMPT

July 9 - 9:28 a.m.

24.62 miles / 5,981 feet

15 hours, 35 minutes

"The hardest walk is walking alone,
but it's also the strongest."

-Anonymous

YESTERDAY, the battery on my phone did not charge. I have a battery charging phone case and used my battery pack to charge it last night. After ten minutes, I learned that the battery pack was not charging my phone case but draining the life from my battery. I removed the battery case from my phone and used what little life was left from my battery packs. It only charged to forty percent, and I still have a few days left before reaching Stevens Pass. From there, I can charge all my electronics at the ski resort. I hope I have just enough battery left on my phone to make it. If I could see the trail, I wouldn't have to use my phone so much. Today, I will turn my phone to the dimmest setting and try not to use it so often.

The trail markers remain hidden well beneath the snow. I end up having to use my phone's map more times than I hoped. By noon, my phone stands at twenty percent power. I do my best to follow other hikers' footprints, but even those remain too fuzzy to follow. The prints disappear entirely in some places. When I lose sight of them, I have to stop and examine the trail for any trace of prints. And when I spot them, their footprints seem to backtrack. This is both confusing and time consuming. *How could I be such an idiot?* I mentally beat myself up for not conserving my battery power better or noticing what was happening with my phone's charging case sooner. There's no turning back and nothing more I can do. I continue on as the miles tick off slowly and tediously. The sun begins to set, and I start worrying the tracks I am following will be lost in the wind. If it rains tonight, I am in major trouble. I decide that no matter how late it gets, I will follow them for as long as possible. Night soon sets in, so I pull out my headlamp and continue following the tracks. I stop and give thanks for the visible prints. I have been following them for days and want to thank whoever made them.

I slip and fall, needing to self-arrest for the second time on the trail. It is pitch black outside, and I cannot see anything below me. I missed my chance to stab my ice axe into the snow because I slid into a tree before I could raise it. I thank the tree for rescuing me. I shine my headlamp up towards where I slipped. This time my ice axe is still in hand; only my trekking pole is what lies above. I slowly work my way back up towards it as adrenaline courses through my veins. *No big deal*, I tell myself, *take your time. I slipped because I was trying to move too fast.*

Remember, slow is smooth, smooth is fast. I continue shining my light up and down the trail, trying to stay on track. My phone is now at ten percent, but the worry of getting lost soon fades as I look up at the sky. Stars shine bright, twinkling a magical dance around the moon and lighting up my trail. I take a deep breath and turn off my headlamp. I look up in awe and wonder. The magnitude of the sky makes me feel so small. A big smile spreads across my face. Peace overcomes me. I turn my head-lamp back on and continue to hike until I make it to another snow-free area.

By two, I finally finish setting up my tent for the night. I grab a few sticks, placing them on the ground in the shape of an ar-row. The arrow points to the direction I will need to continue towards in the morning. I learned this neat trick from the Race Director at the Bigfoot 200-mile ultra. She suggested that if you decide to nap during the race, place an arrow to where you need to go. She said that sometimes you wake up disoriented, and the arrow will help prevent backtracking or getting lost. I really hope I don't get lost tomorrow.

CHAPTER 15

DAY 7 FKT ATTEMPT

July 10 - 9:41 a.m.

19.3 miles / 3,638 feet plus?

"I am not lost, I'm exploring."

-Jana Stanfield

I HAVE GROWN TIRED of wet and blistered feet. When I get out of bed this morning, I decide to keep my long dry socks on. Even though they will get wet from my soaked shoes, I don't care. I slept near a water stream last night. Before setting off for the day, I stop at the stream to filter water. I then take my dirty wet socks and begin to wash them. Days of filth begin to wash away. Instead of sticking them back into the side mesh of my pack where they may not dry, I decide to hang them on the outside. I grab my tiny pocket knife and open up the scissors stored inside. I make tiny holes on the calf end of my socks, and I weave the holes onto my tent poles in the back of my pack, allowing them to hang freely.

I make my way up to Grizzly Peak, mile 174. I get one last look at my phone before it dies. I try to turn it back on. It flashes a plug-in sign and goes blank. My watch starts to beep, telling me to charge it. Eight percent battery life is all that remains. My watch is also too low to scroll to the compass. I pull out my paper map. The Army taught me land navigation, but it isn't easy to get a grip on my location without a compass. Even so, it is only a paper map. With a compass, it would still be nearly impossible to find my way. I begin thinking about what I was taught during land navigation courses, such as looking for prominent features and remembering where I just came from. I make it a mental note that if I look around and don't find my way, I will come back to where I first began.

Why does the PCT have to be under snow? I walk back and forth, searching for any glimpse of the trail. I see nothing. I don't feel scared, but calm, as though I know everything is going to be alright. *I am not lost. I can't be. I am just adventuring with purpose,* I think to myself.

My Garmin inReach has sixteen percent battery life, and I try to send a message. I am supposed to meet my sister today at Stevens Pass. She will hang out with me for a few hours while my electronics charge at the ski resort. I am only twelve miles away, but I'm not sure I'll find my way. Maybe she can hike up and come to my rescue. With my phone dead, I have to message directly on the inReach. Crafting a message means tediously scrolling to each letter when making words. I try to make it short and to the point. I don't even add spaces. I send her the following messages, "Cometometwelveout," and "Cantfindmywayontrail." Sending both messages starts to drain the battery. Fifteen minutes have passed, and the inReach is still trying to send them. I decide to forgo my messages and turn it off because I may need it later.

It is only noon, and I have several hours of daylight left. I make a promise to myself. If I don't find my way out of here by tonight, I will set up camp and try again in the morning. If I still don't see my way by noon tomorrow, I will press my SOS button on my SPOT device. The SOS button would then send a distress signal to inform local responders of my whereabouts. It lets them know I need rescuing. Thinking about this makes me feel guilty and selfish, that I am using up precious resources. I need to find my way!

I begin searching again. My foot sinks into a hole. I reach down and dig a bigger hole around where I had stepped. I found the trail! With this small glimmer of hope, I begin stomping my way forward. The snow has melted underneath, allowing each step to create a hole onto the trail. I don't care if I have to stomp my way down this entire mountain so long as I am on the correct path. But hope fades quickly. After ten steps, my feet no longer sink into the snow. If someone was watching me from a distance, I am sure they would get a kick out of my movements. It looks like I am throwing some type of tantrum stomping atop this mountain in every direction you can imagine. I even stab my trekking pole into the snow all around me and still can't find my way. I have no clue where to go next. I make a mental note of where I just came from and begin searching for any other sign of trail—an emblem, a wooden sign, a trail marker, footsteps, the actual trail, anything. I walk to the left of the peak, looking out and around. No trail. I go back to my starting point and hike along the right side of the peak—still, no trail. I return to my starting point. I hike forward. This area leads to a small slope I must climb. I searched that area earlier with no luck.

Maybe I didn't go far enough. Something inside tells me to go back and to hike further up. I listen to my gut, and climb atop the mound. I see faint footprints once again, and let out an enthusiastic, "YES!" I follow them forward. I lose them again. I repeat the same pattern as before. Walk left and look. Come back, search to the right. Every time I catch a small glimpse of the trail, I let out another, "Yes." I do this for hours. I need to get off this mountain because the sun is beginning to set.

I push on, listening to the direction my intuition leads me, having no clue why this is the right way. I pull out my headlamp and nervously hike over snow-covered boulders. I slow my pace so I don't fall into a hole. Before stepping, I make sure to check the snow with my trekking pole in front of me.

Once I am past this section, I encounter fresh bear tracks. They lead towards the opposite direction of where I am going. I still feel calm. It's as though something has a hold of me—my gut, intuition, instinct, or maybe faith. My great grandfather Albert Madplume crosses my mind, and I feel safe. I think my ancestors are helping me. I have never felt so spiritual and connected with the Earth and my people since starting this hike. I feel as though something is guiding me safely on the correct path and off this mountain.

So, focused on finding my way, the hours pass quickly, and I finally decide that I have had enough for today. It is late, and I am not making it to Stevens Pass tonight. My watch died around one in the morning, and I think it has to be at least two by now. I have no idea how many miles I have hiked today nor how many miles I have left to reach Stevens Pass. I've passed my most challenging day on the trail so far. I am physically, mentally, and emotionally exhausted. I set my tent up near a lake, hoping for a better tomorrow. Hoping I don't get lost.

CHAPTER 16

DAY 8 FKT ATTEMPT

July 11 - 9:00 a.m.

11.1 miles / 1,680 feet

13 hours, 39 minutes

"The glory of the day was in her face, the beauty of the night was in her eyes."

-James Weldon Johnson

I AM AWAKENED by two fishermen heading to the lake. With no clue what time it is, I slowly unzip my tent. My sister must be worried by now. I didn't make it to her last night as we had planned. I press the black message button on my SPOT device to send my pre-set message so they know I'm okay.

After dressing and packing up for the day, I commit to getting directions from the fisherman. I hike towards the lake where the men are casting. "Good morning; what lake is this?" I ask.

"Lake Valhalla," the whiskered man replies. This striking icy cold glacier lake near Lichtenburg Mountain and Mount McCausland beams. The lake sits unmoved like glass.

"What trailhead did you come from?" I ask, digging for more information. I sadly find out, not from Stevens Pass. "Do you know how many miles to Stevens Pass?" They do not know. Now a little discouraged, I say, "It's okay, I know I am close. What time is it?" They tell me it is nine. My eyes widen, surprised to find out I'm very late and need to get moving. I wish the gentlemen good luck on fishing today and rush back towards the trail. At this point, with a lot of snow ahead to maneuver around, it will be a slick hike back from where I left off.

I joyfully smile at the trail ahead. There are PCT markers everywhere to follow. I come across several day hikers, which means I am close to the start of the trailhead and Stevens Pass. One hiker informs me I am only three miles away. After a few miles from the lake, it is a nice snowless descent, and for the first time in days, I am worry-free.

Once I finally make it to the trailhead, I search everywhere for my sister. I don't see her, but I need to use the restroom badly. I was hoping for a privy in this area but see none. I make my way up and over the bridge towards Stevens Pass. This site has a privy in the parking lot. I hike towards it. There are a few cars parked near the area, but no one seems to be using them. I soon learn why and am surprised at what I see inside. Unlike the privy at Hart's Pass, this one is in the complete opposite condition. Trash is stacked everywhere. Fecal matter and urine cover the toilet seats and ground. Dirty diapers and glass litter the floor. The stench is even worse. I feel dirty just looking at it and quickly close the door. I guess I will have to go to the bathroom in the woods. As I walk away, a lady walks towards me, and I tell her it is pretty bad in there. She decides to check for herself. She continues to walk towards the door, opens it, looks inside, and shuts it. She quickly walks towards me, smiles, and says, "I will just hold it," while also acknowledging she should have just listened to me.

I make my way a tenth of a mile past the privies to the Stevens Pass ski facility. From here, there are several tables with benches and outlets to charge my things. I plug in everything. I remove my tent from my pack and lay it across a table to dry, and place my socks, shoes, and insoles onto the seats. I grab my extra pair of socks hanging off my tent poles earlier in the day but realize I am missing one. I look around, hoping it has fallen off somewhere near, but it is nowhere. I grab my seat pad, place it on the ground, and sit atop it near my phone. I stretch my legs out and begin to relax. My bare feet enjoy the warmth of the sun and the freedom from shoes.

Once my phone charges, it turns on and starts buzzing like crazy. All my missed messages and texts download at once. My first time on the trail with cell service, I ignore them and call my sister. She waited for me but had to get back home for work, and my mother and dog Lily were also with her. However, my brother has already headed in my direction and should be there in a few hours. I am not in a rush to leave because I need to make sure all my devices charge.

My stomach begins to rumble. If only COVID-19 hadn't happened, I could be eating at the restaurant nearby right now and get a room at the lodge. I grab a snack and begin to munch away as I am checking through my messages. I post a few photos online, call my mom, and text message my friends and family.

I call my friend Rebecca. I met her during the Tahoe 200-mile race back in 2018. She also paced me at the 2019 Franklin Mountain 200 miler by running over 60 miles of the race with me. Her kind, spunky, and energetic attitude helped me win the female division and place fourth overall during that race. She has a Facebook page called "Women of the Mountain," which features female athletes. She does a fantastic job posting my progress on her page, making it one less thing I have to do.

While waiting for my brother, I book a room at Summit Inn in Snoqualmie. I should arrive in two days. A gentleman working as a security guard for Stevens Pass approaches me.

"Hi, are you hiking the PCT?" he asks.

"Yes, I am."

He replies, "I am from the Pacific Crest Trail hiking class of 2015. Which way are you headed?"

"I am headed Southbound."

"Where did you start from?"

"I started from Hart's Pass then hiked up to the Canadian border."

He responds, "Oh, wow! Did you skip any sections?"

I shake my head while happily responding with, "No, I did not."

He looks at me in amazement. "I have only seen two other southbound hikers. They were here yesterday."

I wonder if those are the footprints of the hikers I have been following. The same footprints that helped guide me here, I think to myself.

"Well, you are free to set up camp near the area. I am usually in charge of handling all resupply boxes but because of COVID-19, I could not take resupply this year. Do you need anything?"

Even though my stomach twists with hunger, I say, "No, thank you. I am okay."

I just want to sit down, relax, and finish checking my messages, but he continues to ask questions.

"Do you have a trail name?" he asks.

I say, "No, not yet," as I haven't crossed paths with enough PCT hikers for one of them to give me one.

The husky gentleman ponders, trying to come up with a name for me. At the time, I was sitting around barefoot, so he said, "What about 'Bare Feet?'" I smirk and shake my head no. He then asks where I am from.

"Well, from all over, but born and raised here in Washington."

"Oh, and you're headed southbound?" he asks.

I say, "Yes."

"Well, what about, 'Walks Away,'" he suggests. I chuckle and politely give him another no. "Well, I hope you settle on a good one. If you need anything, I will be here for awhile."

I nod my head in acknowledgment, give him my thanks, and we part ways.

My brother shows up around three that afternoon. He sits with me as I wait for my electronics to finish charging. By now, my watch, Garmin inReach, and headlamp are fully charged. It's the power banks that take forever.

You don't realize how much you yearn for a face-to-face conversation with someone you love until you haven't had one in a while. I don't tell Michael I am hungry, although I know he can see it in my face. My cheeks are sunken in and my pants sag. I haven't bathed in almost two weeks. I must look horrible. I tell him of my adventures so far, and he updates me about my kids. I enjoy our chat and don't want it to end. My brother has a certain loving and kind-hearted way about him. His drive here involves an eight-hour round trip to sit with me for four hours. My sister and mother drove about the same. That's the kind of family I have. We are all very close. We love to joke and tease one another and are always looking out for each other.

Our mother primarily raised us. Growing up, she was our biggest cheerleader. She taught us to love nature, be bold, and push ourselves. As a nurse, she worked hard to provide us with everything we needed. She made sure we were involved in sports to learn all the values that come along with them. Her work ethic and ability to care for others also taught us empathy, compassion, and love for humankind. My father, a farmer, has the same passion for nature. He taught us to respect the animals and the land. He also taught me the importance of not taking things for granted and to always leave an area better than when I arrived.

Although I don't want my brother to leave, I know I should get going. My two power banks aren't fully charged, but I feel it's enough to get me through the next two days until I reach Snoqualmie Pass. I finally leave at seven. Michael walks a quarter of a mile with me before having to turn around. He gives me a big hug and asks if he can pray over me. This catches me by surprise. I hold back tears, letting his words sink in. There is a strength to his prayer. I will never forget this moment and wish I could memorize his every word. He asks the creator to watch over and protect me along my journey. He knows I will respect the animals I cross paths with and asks that they do the same. Motivating me to keep pushing, he tells me I am doing great with one giant hug, and he will meet me at Snoqualmie Pass in a few days.

I hike for another hour before it starts to pour. *Ahh,* Washington State and all of its rain. I stop to put on all my rain gear and crampons. I had planned to hike just another hour, but fresh mountain lion tracks in the snow give me an eerie feeling. I keep going until I can no longer see them. It is overcast out, and the rain makes it feel as though I am walking in clouds. Even with my headlamp on, the fog makes visibility minimal. By ten-thirty, I've committed to all I can for the day. I find the perfect location underneath some trees to set up my tent, and I manage to block most of the wind and rain. It is near Josephine Lake, mile 193.3. Hopefully, the fog clears up, and I can get a good look at the lake in the morning.

CHAPTER 17

DAY 9 FKT ATTEMPT

July 12 - 7:07 a.m.

33.61 miles / 6,588 feet

16 hours, 38 minutes

"Words have meaning and names have power."

-Anonymous

TODAY'S GOAL IS THIRTY TO THIRTY-THREE MILES. I have sixty-six miles left to go to reach Snoqualmie Pass and just enough food to make it there. It rained sizably last night, and this morning is no different. Hearing the raindrops hit my tent, I put my rain pants and rain jacket on before exiting. I feel a bit disappointed that it is too foggy to get a view of Josephine Lake. By ten-thirty, the rain starts to clear. The fog lifts, allowing the mountains to peak out of hiding. Although I find myself playing the crampons on-and-off game, the beautiful day keeps my spirits high.

I begin thinking about the conversation I had about my trail name with the husky gentlemen at Stevens Pass yesterday. Traditionally, other hikers bestow a trail name to you. A trail name can be silly, serious, or related to one's hiking experience. A trail name does not have to be original, and more than one person can share the same name. Once decided upon, that is how you introduce yourself to other hikers. A hiker also doesn't have to have a trail name if they don't want one.

My thoughts then shift toward my Indian name. I use it often in prayer and for strength and courage. Since I won't be seeing many hikers, I decided not to wait to be given a name and will use my Indian name as my trail name. It was given to me by Chief Earl Oldperson of the Blackfeet Tribe in 2008.

When I returned home from Iraq, my family and I visited our relatives in Browning, Montana. Upon arrival, I learned my Aunt Minnie and mother had secretly set up a ceremony for me during my deployment. They escorted me to Chief Earl Oldperson's office. As I entered, he stood to welcome me. I felt at ease and grasped tightly onto his every word. At the age of seventy-eight, he was considered a prominent elder and political leader of the Blackfeet tribe. His wisdom, understanding, and kindness radiated throughout the room. We both took a seat as he asked what I enjoyed doing in life and what made me happy. At the time, I was only twenty-three years old. While in the Army, part of my training included Airborne training, which resulted in me becoming a paratrooper for the 82nd Airborne Division. Training allowed me to parachute out of perfectly good flying airplanes. I also earned my Air Assault badge, which gave me the opportunity to become certified towards rappelling from helicopters. Before deployment, I had been working on getting my skydiving license. I loved the feeling of flying high up and viewing the Earth's curvature. The vast views and surge of adrenaline express what I had enjoyed most.

The Chief gave me a big smile as I told him about my passion. It was then that he decided on a name for me. Only, it was up to me to accept it. As the words Isht' Putaki (phonetically sounding _eesht potakee_) were softly spoken from his mouth, a wave of emotion flooded over me. I smiled from ear to ear and loved everything about my new, flawless name. How could I not accept this wonderful gift? In return, the Chief offered me an eagle feather and some sweet grass. I would return with his offering in hand to a hall filled with friends and family, some whom I had never even met. I proudly said to myself, _THIS IS MY TRIBE_, and _THESE ARE MY PEOPLE_. Although I was never raised on the Blackfeet reservation, it didn't matter. They accepted me for me.

At this moment, gratitude and love ruled over my thoughts. As we stood there listening to the wise words from the Chief, a drummer and singer soon started a traditional song. As though my jaw had dropped, I was amazed by the beauty of the music—what an incredible gift. The Chief turned to me. It was my turn to give a speech, but I was not prepared. I tried to show how grateful I was and could not thank them enough. I felt proud of my name. I never thought something so simple as a name could have such power.

At the time, I thought I earned this name simply because of my love for jumping out of planes. But as time continues to pass, I have found several meanings behind the name given to me. To fly high means to prosper and prosperity comes from the lessons I have learned along the way. Sometimes I envision myself soaring above the clouds as though I am actually flying. I get the same feeling from climbing a mountain. Over the years, Isht' Putaki has given me strength and courage. I find myself often reciting my name, Isht' Putaki, throughout my days. I decide that from here on out, my trail name will be Isht' Putaki, which translates to Flys High Woman. I will go by "Flys High" to make things simpler.

As I continue on with my hike and am pleased I have decided on a trail name, I can't help but notice all the water I have been passing today. Every lake is just as gorgeous as the next. I especially enjoy the baby-blue-colored water surrounded by snow and evergreens. I have always gravitated towards blues and greens. Being able to see both in one setting over and over again is a dream come true. I love it up here. I am not bothered by the number of downed trees I am forced to climb over and around on this section. Although these mountains are tough to climb, my efforts vanish by the reward awaiting with each peak. The forest seems to have no end. It stretches on forever. Lakes in the distance and the vastness of trees always bring a huge smile to my face. This experience is heavenly. I don't want to leave the top of each mountain I climb, but I must.

I scramble down towards a creek at mile 211.5. Out of all the water crossings I have made, this one is by far the most difficult. It is a large rocky creek full of fast-flowing white water. The water breaks into smaller streams leaving just enough unexposed rock to hopscotch my way across. I begin to make my way to the other side of the trail, but a powerful stream quickly turns me back to my starting point. I spot some cairns further down the creek and hike towards them. The flow is much stronger and wider in this area. Someone must have placed the perfectly stacked rocks there last year because there is no way I could safely cross from this point. I turn back and take my chances further up.

Luckily, someone has also placed cairns up ahead. I head towards them, crossing smaller water streams in the process. My shoes become soaked once again. The cairns are on top of a huge boulder just on the other side of the last wide stream I need to cross. The water is fast flowing but just narrow enough for me to jump over. I take a deep breath, and with a burst of energy, I make the giant leap. My body slams into the boulder of cairns, slicing a small piece of skin off my finger and snapping my trekking pole in two. Grateful I have made it safely; I don't even care I am bleeding. I am just happy I made it across.

I find a nice piece of dirt to kneel on and begin to open my pack. I reach towards the bottom of it and pull out my first aid kit. I grab a Band-Aid and duct tape. Thankfully the pole snapped towards the top so that I can repair it. I continue hiking, crossing paths with a female hiker heading northbound. We update one another about the conditions ahead and quickly return towards our separate ways. I think about how many backpackers I have seen, and surprisingly, I have come across more females than males.

I smell fire. It is a strong odor and easily identifiable. The trail leads me right towards the source. Four young men are sitting near a campfire with their tents already set up for the night. As I pass, we don't say a word to one another. Instead, I keep my eyes on the trail and continue on my way.

The trail eventually leads me towards the top of this climb near Peggy's Pond. There is a giant boulder overlooking the pond called Cathedral Rock. For some reason, it reminds me of Chief Mountain in Montana, a mountain located on the Blackfeet Indian Reservation. It is something I have always longed to climb. *Maybe this is my Chief Mountain,* I say to myself. Once I make it past Peggy's Pond, I am excited for the easy descent that awaits. I feel like I am flying as my pace picks up going down. With every step, the pounding in my quadriceps begins to intensify with pain, but I don't care. My legs are tired anyway, and I am having too much fun running down.

Once I make it towards the bottom, it isn't long before I enter an area full of much taller shrubs than my five-foot-four frame. As the minutes pass, my quadriceps ache even more. My feet feel as though someone has pounded a hammer to them and I am walking on nails. Each step strains as painfully as the next, slowing my pace dramatically. I am ready to stop, set up camp, and elevate them, but I have to keep going. The nearest designated backcountry campsite is three miles away, which means at least another hour and a half left of hiking. The shrubs have made the trail too narrow to set up a tent. I wouldn't say I like hiking in this type of terrain, especially at night. Usually, I enjoy night hiking but seeing bear scat on several parts of the trail makes me weary. I have to keep going. I have to make it to an area wide and safe enough to set up my tent.

Statistically, I know that you have a greater chance of trip-
ping on a pebble and dying than getting attacked by a bear. In
fact, over the past 150 years, there has only been one document-
ed death caused by a black bear in the wilderness of California,
Washington, and Oregon. I know the statistics, and I know my
odds. But when you are walking alone in the woods at night,
your thoughts dangerously wander, especially as the density of
the trail increases.

When I finally make it near the campsite, I stop on the trail. I
pull out my bear bag and hike toward the opposite side of
where I will be setting up my tent for the night. Once I find a
tree to secure my bear bag, I hobble back to the trail, finally
making my way to camp, mile 224.9. I set my tent up as quickly
as possible and slowly crawl inside.

The unbearable pain in my feet starts to make me feel nauseous. I take my time untying my wet shoes and gingerly pull
them off my feet, wincing in pain. Then I pull off my socks and
bandages one by one. Each foot looks swollen and blistered. I
sit for over thirty minutes, massaging each foot. I nod off to
sleep a few times but wake up suddenly when I feel like I am
falling over.

I start shivering. I know the temperature is dropping quickly, and I have to set up my sleeping quilt and pad for the night.
All I pine for is a work-free night and to feel the inside warmth
of my quilt. I try mustering the energy to finish setting up.
With chattered teeth and goose-bumped arms, I open my
backpack and pull out what I need. I put on my base layers,
puffy jacket, place my neck gaiter over my ears and begin to

air up my mattress. It feels remarkable being able to finally crawl into the comfort of my sleeping quilt.

I massage my feet again and try to elevate them by propping them up onto my backpack. I am incredibly uncomfortable trying to sleep on my back. Months of wearing armor and over a dozen airborne jumps in the military messed my back up. I sleep far better on my side, and if I continue to lay on my back, it means waking up to additional back pain in the morning. I toss and turn but cannot get comfortable. My swollen feet throb so much, preventing me from falling asleep. I just want them to stop hurting. I want the swelling and the achiness to go away. At this point, I would rather be in labor than deal with this torment.

It is then I decide to do the one thing you should never do when sleeping. I would sleep with my feet on the upside and my head on the downside. Since I set up my tent on a slant, all I have to do is just turn my sleeping pad and quilt around. It seems to help a lot. I feel the fluid from my feet slowly pulling away, providing some relief. I just hope I wake up tomorrow without regretting my decision to sleep this way.

CHAPTER 18

DAY 10 & 11 FKT ATTEMPT

July 13 & 14 - 9:17 a.m.

36.16 miles / 8,317 feet

19 hours, 20 minutes

"When my legs hurt, I say:
'Shut up legs! Do what I tell you to do!'"

-Jens Voigt

MORNING ARRIVES QUICKLY, and I take the covers off my feet. The swelling has decreased significantly, but my face feels puffy. I pull out my phone to take a look. My entire face, especially around my eyes, is swollen. The fluid has shifted to my head. Always optimistic, I had hoped this wouldn't happen. I don't regret my decision to sleep that way. It was a small price to pay to be able to finally fall asleep. I snap a photo to show my husband and begin to pack up for the day.

I am still physically drained and running low on fumes. Yesterday's hike has taken a lot out of me, and my face's swelling makes me feel groggy. I slowly get dressed and pack up my sleeping quilt and sleeping pad. I place a few fresh bandages along with some Trail Toes over the blisters on my feet and slip my one dry sock onto my left foot because it looks the worst.

I look at my wet shoes with disdain. After last night, I don't want to put them on. I take a deep breath and grab them, slowly sliding my feet into their wet and soggy soles. I unzip my tent and peer out. The sun is shining. I crawl out of the tent and onto my feet. My quadriceps are incredibly sore today. I walk 200 feet to the opposite side of the trail to get my bear bag. I return to my tent and take a seat. I rub each leg and give them a pep talk as if trying to coax them into crushing today's hike. *C'mon legs, just one more day, and then I will treat you to a warm meal and a bath.* Of course, this does nothing. They feel the same: tired and sore. Maybe I just need more sleep. I didn't make it to camp until late last night. I know I need more food. I have just enough calories to get me through today and to reach Summit Inn at Snoqualmie Pass where my first resupply package awaits. I've filled my re-supply with Epsom salts and a six-day supply of food.

I will stop at the gas station next to the hotel tomorrow morning and pick up additional food items. I know I have lost weight. I am in a calorie deficit and should have packed more food. I didn't prepare for the extra days it is taking me to reach the Summit Inn.

It's hard not to fixate on food when you barely have any. I can't wait to order a meal at the hotel's restaurant. I'm hoping it's open despite COVID-19 mandated closures. I can't help but daydream about all of the food possibilities. What will I eat first? A gallon of ice cream, waffles, a burger, French fries, steak, eggs? I want it all. My stomach starts to rumble over the thought of a warm meal that is not dehydrated. I need to eat breakfast. I grab my stove to boil water. I have two packets of oatmeal left. I will eat both of them throughout my morning. I am all out of coffee. I grab what's left of my food and set it aside for the day. It's not much; a bar, half a bag of Pasta Primavera, half a packet of Silverstar Nutrition's Chocolate Protein Powder, and half a bag of Apple Crisp. I try to calculate just how many calories this food will provide but soon give up. It doesn't matter. It's very little, and I need to get moving. Once my tent is packed up, and everything is in its proper place, I pick up my bag of oatmeal and begin to eat and hike. It is a cool morning, and I am thankful for my Ziploc-filled bag of warm oatmeal. It warms my hands and fills my stomach.

After finishing half of my breakfast, I store it in the front of my hip belt pocket. I need to spread my calories out as best as possible if I am going to make it through today. I slowly start to pick up my pace. The thought of all the food I will have at my disposal tomorrow is my motivation to hike just a little bit faster.

I only need thirty-five miles to make it to the Summit Inn. I easily wrap my mind around the thought of that distance. My fastest 50k race to date is just under five hours. I wish I had the energy to run up and over this mountain. I wish I could get anywhere close to that time. I know my hiking pace, and my body is weak from lack of food. My legs also respond in disagreement. They are extremely sore, especially my quadriceps, and it took some time to get them going today. I haven't even mentioned my feet. Although achy, they are nowhere near as bad as they were last night. Days of hiking in soaking wet shoes and the extra weight of my snow gear have destroyed them.

I am now ten miles in and climbing. The swelling in my face continues making me feel groggy and sleepy. The temperature has also warmed up, causing me to overheat. I stop next to a huge boulder. I prop each leg up one at a time and roll my pant legs up just below my knees. I take my sweater off and stuff it into the side mesh of my pack. I begin to hike again. I am still feeling sleepy. I just need coffee or something to wake me up. I quickly regret my thoughts as my right leg screams in agony.

I am on a trail full of beautiful flowers. Unavoidable, my legs brush up against them, disturbing where bees are collecting pollen. "OUCH!" I yell as a stinger enters my calf. I quickly stop and take it out. Adrenaline pumps through my body, and I pick up my pace to move as far away from these bee-infested flowers as possible. Although I could have done without the bee sting, I had wished for something to wake me up this morning. The saying, *"bee" careful what you wish for*, crosses my mind, making me chuckle a little.

Once I reach mile 241, I am amazed at the amount of water coming off the side of the mountain. It is the biggest waterfall I have seen on the PCT. A manmade bridge allows me to cross the Delate Creek safely, and I stop in the middle of it to admire its beauty. Water splashes onto my face while I record a video to share with my kids.

Another mile, the pain in my legs starts to become unbearable once again, just as they had during yesterday's hike. It is difficult not to fixate on the pain when there is nothing else to distract me. Trying to save the battery life on my phone and power banks, I have yet to listen to any music or audiobooks. I pre-downloaded a few before my journey. I need a distraction, though, and I know I have enough battery life to make it a few days before needing a recharge. Since I will be hitting Snoqualmie today, I decide to turn up the speaker on my phone and drown out my pain with an audiobook. It's a nice distraction and a much-needed morale booster. After two hours, I turn it off and refocus on the task at hand. From here, the mountain becomes a roller coaster taking my emotions along for the ride.

As I begin another ascent, the sun starts to set. Throughout my journey, I have seen a lot of beauty in nature. Only this time, the view catches me off guard. The view of Mount Rainier in the distance is breathtaking. I am high up, and shades of reds and blues surround Mount Rainier. The power that this mountain is emitting is overwhelming. I begin to weep. Not of sadness nor sorrow but of pure happiness. For, in this moment, I am not concerned about the pain in my legs nor the rumbling in my stomach. I am grateful. I thank Mother Earth for showing me all her beauty and can't wait to see what the rest of my journey entails.

I finally make it to Alaska Mountain, which will be my last climb of the night. Before I start my ascent, I cross paths with two hikers setting up camp. They look to be in their late forties or early fifties.

"Hello, how's it going?" I introduce myself to them.

"We are hanging in there," one man replies. "Where are you coming from?"

"Twenty-five miles back," I tell them. They look at me in shock. "What about you guys? Were are you headed?"

"We just came from Snoqualmie Pass and are headed to Stevens Pass. Do you need anything to eat?"

I must look starved, I think to myself. I decline twice, but the men insist.

I am about to decline their generosity a third time when one of the gentlemen responds with a bag of goodies in hand. "I have dark chocolates."

These just so happen to be my favorite chocolates on Earth. I can't resist. I take a few steps forward, reaching my hand up towards the chocolates.

The man says, "You can have the entire bag." They chuckle at the gratitude in my voice.

"Oh, thank you so much!"

Darkness is setting in quickly. They ask, "Will you be making this next climb tonight?"

They must be fathers because their concern is both kind and genuine, reminding me of my own.

I tell them, "Yes, I am continuing on tonight."

"Do you have microspikes? The two fellow hikers we had seen earlier had nothing on for traction."

"I saw them too. That is so dangerous. I do have microspikes, but I also have crampons and will be using those to make this climb."

We say our farewells; I thank them for the chocolates once again and set off.

The trail is challenging to follow because of the number of

tracks heading in different directions. I continue to hike and pull out my phone to check the trail. It is a slow climb. Once I make it to the top, I tell myself that it will be a quick descent down. The peak is windy, and I can see lights from a town far off in the distance. I turn my phone back on, hoping that it connects to the town's satellites. Just as predicted, it begins to chime. I hike 100 yards down and out of the wind, find a rock, and sit. I take off my crampons and call my brother. No answer. I call my mom. She picks up on the first ring. "Hello, Mom."

"Hi, Jess," my mom says excitedly. "How are you? Where are you?"

I tell her I am doing fine, just ten miles from the Summit Inn. It is eight o'clock. I should be there by midnight. This next section should be quick because it is a 4,000-foot descent, which means almost no more climbing.

She tells me that my brother is out hiking and is planning to meet me on the trail to hike into town with me. "Really?" I ask in excitement. I hang up and text my brother. Minutes later, he has service and calls me back.

"Where are you, sis?" he asks.

"I am just under ten miles from the Summit Inn. How far are you, Michael?"

He tells me he is about one mile from the trailhead. "Okay, great," I say. "We should be able to link up somewhere around the five-mile mark," I tell him. We both hang up. I grab a dark chocolate and stuff it into my mouth. *Man, this tastes amazing.* The chocolate is frozen, making it crunchy. When I am home, I always place my chocolate into the freezer. It is my favorite way to eat them, and the cold temperatures tonight have made them equally hard. I then grab two chocolates and eat them both at the same time. They taste even better.

As I am munching away on the chocolates, I pull out my headlamp and pick up the pace. I hike a quarter of a mile and reach an enormous snow mound blocking the trail. A tunnel has melted through it, so I hike under it. The tunnel soon comes to an end, and there is no way through. I turn around, forced to hike alongside the trail over the snow. I pull out my crampons and unhook my ice axe once again. I fold up one trekking pole and stuff it in my pack.

I move to the side of the trail and look around, searching for the safest route possible. I can see where others have traveled, so I lower myself to the ground and begin scooting toward their footprints. Off to one side is an opening where the snow weakened and fell through, leaving a huge hole in place. I pray the snow is solid enough to hold me and there are no crevices to fall into.

I continue to follow the footsteps, poking the snow in front of me with my trekking pole. Once I reach the other side, I remove my crampons again, but not for long. I turn the corner, and all I see is more snow angled against the side of the mountain. For the next three miles, I have no choice but to wear my crampons. My pace slows significantly. My brother has reached the five-mile marker and calls me. "Where you at, sis?" he asks.

"I am sorry. I am only three miles from where we last spoke," I say. "I have to trudge through so much snow, and I have to wear my crampons. Sorry, I am moving so slow."

He says, "It's okay; our paths will eventually cross." I take a deep breath and forge forward.

The crampons pinch my feet so much that they are throbbing in pain. Chocolate distracts me. I save a dark chocolate for my brother. I want him to enjoy the same deliciousness. I am so hungry, though, and soon give in to temptation. I eat mine, and then I eat the chocolate I had been saving for him. Guilty that it is my last chocolate, I take my time trying to savor every bit of it.

It is another slow mile with more snow to traverse before I finally see my brother. He is on the other side of a massive mound of ice. I yell, "Hello!"

He loudly responds, "I don't have the proper gear to hike across the ice, so I will wait here for you."

I slowly hike towards him, stabbing my ice axe into the snow for safety and balance. Once we connect, my brother tells me there are two more snowy sections we need to pass, and then it's easy going from there, and I can take off my crampons. Once we finally make it past those sections, I rest.

We both comment about the huge light coming from the distance. I thought it was a building at first. My brother said he thought it was my headlamp until he realized what it was. He tells me that it's Comet Neowise, and it will not visit Earth for another 6,700 years! We both try to take a picture of it from our phones, but it does not capture the sheer magnitude. We stare in awe and chat about it as we start our hike into town. In reality, it's more of my brother schooling me on space and comets, which has always been a passion of his.

We are four miles away from reaching the Summit Inn. My legs start to feel weak. This descent is unbearably torturous. As though my body has officially turned into molasses, I slow my pace way down. I stop and take a seat. If I could, I would camp here for the night, but I need to make it to the Inn where my kids are waiting. I tell my brother that I am in so much pain and that having to hike downhill is hurting my quadriceps. He asks if I have any medicine to take. I have two packets of Tylenol 500 in my first aid kit. With a worried look on his face, he tells me I should take it. Up until this point, I had been avoiding any pain relievers because of my bout with rhabdomyolysis in February.

Although hesitant, I take the Tylenol and can't wait for it to kick in. An hour passes, and still nothing; I feel the same. With every step, the pain grows, forcing me to stop several times along the way. I am determined to make it, though. It is two in the morning, and we only have two miles to go. But each mile takes an hour. Even though my brother is a good conversationalist, it does nothing to distract me from the pain. He knows I am suffering and tries his best to cheer me up.

He tells me about my kids and how amazing they have been. He tells me about how the family is doing and talks about his work. My responses are nothing more than a few short replies and nods. He is so patient and understanding and tells me to take as much time as I need.

We finally make it to the road that leads to the Summit Inn. It is now four in the morning, and I have been painstakingly hiking for well over twenty hours now. I am exhausted. We pass a gas station, closed for the night. I just want food! I will have to wait a few hours before I can pick up my resupply box. At this point, I don't care. All I want to do is lie down. Luckily, there is a vending machine close to our room. I grab my room key, and as we walk towards it, my brother points to a door near ours, informing me that my kids and stepdad are sleeping in there. When I enter my room, I drop my pack on the floor. I begin digging through it, tossing everything out until I have reached the bottom. "What are you doing?" my brother asks. "I am looking for my money to go buy food from the vending machine," I say. He laughs. He knows I cannot accept anything from him, and he did not want to tempt me, so he says he does not have any food on him.

I find my money and hobble barefoot, straight to the vending machine. I have enough dollar bills to buy a soda and two bags of chips. I head back to the room and lie on the bed. My brother is already sound asleep on the twin bed next to me. I lie there, still in my hiking clothes, devouring both bags of potato chips. I take a few chugs of my soda and doze off.

I wake up a few hours later to knocking at the door. It is my kids, excited to see me. We talk for a while, and then I tell them I need to pick up my resupply box and take a bath. I shuffle my way up to the front desk to get my package with my kids next to me. Once I am back in my room, I open my resupply box and pull out a bag of Epsom salt. I start some bath water and dump the entire bag into the tub. As I grab a few snacks from my resupply box, my kids return to their room with my stepfather Johnny. I re-enter the bathroom, setting my snacks next to the tub. I don't want to look at myself in the mirror yet, so I slowly lower my body into the warm water. I let out a giant sigh. The bath feels amazing. Once I finish my snacks, I place a hand towel below my neck, and my body begins to relax.

I haven't bathed in fourteen days. I close my eyes and slowly drift off. An hour later, I hear a knock at the door. "Are you okay in there?" my brother asks.

I respond, "Yes, just fell asleep." The water has turned cold, so I open the drain to empty the tub and turn on the shower. The water feels even more incredible than before, so refreshing and warm. I try never to take for granted a warm shower. I grab a hand towel and begin to scrub my face then legs. There is so much filth caked on them it turns the towel brown.

When I am finally clean, I wrap a towel around my hair and look into the mirror. My stomach is sunken in; I've lost so much weight. My arms and face look so thin. My hips are bruised from cinching down my pack so tight. I look frail. It reminds me of the Naked and Afraid television show survivalists when they have made it to the end of their twenty-one-day challenge. The difficulties of hunting and gathering food cause them to lose an absurd amount of weight.

I slowly begin dressing. I put my Smartwool sleep clothing and down jacket on and exit the bathroom. I bundle up my dirty clothes and shoes. Still hobbling and barefoot, I take them to the laundry room and toss them in the washer. I return to my kids' room, and we all walk to the hotel's restaurant together. I am famished! I look over the menu. I want to eat everything on it but settle for waffles, eggs, bacon, and coffee. Because of eating so little for over a week, it is difficult to eat it all. I box up what is left to munch on throughout the day. I spend the rest of the morning hanging out with my kids, drying out my gear, and finishing my laundry. I also do a better job fixing the slit on my pack from the day I left the Northern Terminus. I remove the duct tape and repair it with the needle and thread from my first aid kit.

My brother and I walk back over to the gas station at lunchtime to grab food for everyone. We buy burritos and jojo potatoes, and then I shop for myself. I spend over forty dollars on gas station food. I don't settle for small bags of chips and drinks, but buy the biggest size of foods I can find, including giant bags of jalapeno chips, lemon-lime potato chips, double stuffed Oreos, one gallon of mint chocolate chip ice cream, beef jerky, soda, carbonated water, a burrito, and some jojo potatoes.

We return to the room, and I begin eating the mint chocolate chip ice cream before it melts. I share the ice cream with my kids, and we all enjoy it together. I open the bag of potato chips, and we munch on those too. I polish off the burrito, jojo potatoes, soda, and carbonated water.

I still feel weak. My legs are still sore, and my feet are incredibly swollen. I elevate them and continue talking with my kids. I decide that after hiking until four this morning, I need more sleep, but I also want to spend more time with them. I told them I would stay for the remainder of the day and leave first thing tomorrow morning. We eat dinner at the restaurant, and I place all the leftover food from the store into Ziploc bags. I will eat it all on the trail tomorrow. I make sure that this time, I will not run out of food.

That night, I sleep with my feet elevated on pillows. They are so swollen you can't see my ankles. My toes remind me of tiny sausages. Tapping into our dark humor once again, my brother and I laugh at how swollen and pitiful my feet look. My youngest daughter cuddles next to me for the rest of the night. As I begin to doze off, I can't help but wonder if I will feel better tomorrow.

CHAPTER 19

DAY 12 FKT ATTEMPT

July 15 - 8:10 a.m.

30.46 miles / 6,775 feet

13 hours, 24 minutes

"Injuries are our best teachers."

-Scott Jurek

I AM AWAKE BY SEVEN and take my time getting ready. The mountains have kicked my butt these past weeks. I will have to average almost forty-seven miles per day now in order to beat Scott's record. I don't even know if that's possible, but I am still optimistic.

Although I am happy because I could pick up my resupply box and buy extra food from the gas station yesterday, I am not excited about the added weight that comes with it. I also can't ditch the crampons, microspikes, ice axe, stove, and extra winter clothes quite yet. According to the PCT Facebook pages and weather forecasts, there is still snow ahead.

Once I leave the Inn, I make one last stop at the gas station. I buy a breakfast burrito, a bag of mini chocolate donuts, and a cup of coffee. I walk across the road and back onto the trail. It was difficult to leave my kids, even with the funny pep talk about kicking butt they gave me this morning. I continue to look back at the Inn, hoping to get one last look at them peeking out the window. I then make the 650-foot climb over one mile as the Inn disappears from sight.

When I finally reach the top and begin descending, my legs start to feel as rough as they had the previous day hiking with my brother. The pain in my quadriceps starts to become unbearable, and I am only seven miles in for the day. I message my husband about how terrible I am feeling. To my surprise, he responds. He tells me to sit down and rest for a while. He also tells me that I better be peeing like a racehorse. Come to think of it, I haven't had to use the restroom much today. I stop and chug two bottles of water. I know dehydration can trigger rhabdomyolysis. This proves true because within thirty minutes, the pain in my legs begins to disappear and my legs begin to feel better.

Only having to ever deal with rhabdomyolysis once before, I completely missed the signs. Even when I was hesitant to take Tylenol, it hadn't dawned on me that the weakness in my legs was a sign. Up until that moment, I had thought the fatigue was from days of hiking in relentless terrain and weather. I message my husband that I am feeling better and the water has helped. I start to think about how much water I had actually been drinking since the start of the trail. The answer is not much. How could I be so dumb? Why hadn't I caught this before? I didn't stick to my usual rule of a minimum of one bottle of water every morning while hiking. From this moment on, I promise myself that I will chug a bottle of water every morning before the start of my day's hike. I will also drink a bottle of water a few miles before setting up camp in the evening. I will make it a point to drink water all day, every day.

Although there is an improvement with how my legs are feeling, they are completely trashed. Rhabdomyolysis involves the breakdown of muscle tissue, and I am paying for my mistake of not drinking enough water. I am lucky I caught the problem early on before something worse like kidney failure happened. While I am not in the same amount of pain I was in before, my legs continue to be extremely sore. They feel like I just crushed a killer leg day at the gym.

By evening, the weight of my backpack feels as though I have spent my day carrying a bag of bricks. Even worse, I cannot find my hoodie, which has been my favorite piece of trail gear. The campsite I chose for the night gives me one bar of service. It also has one of the only streams for the next eight miles. Located at mile 289.1, the stream is a short distance from the trail, but I don't mind the added walk. I hike to it and fill up all my water bottles so that I won't have extra work in the morning.

I message back and forth with my husband directly from my phone. I also message my brother hoping that I may have left my hoodie in the hotel room. Michael messages me back. He tells me he couldn't find it. Even though I am saddened that I must have lost it somewhere along the way, I am happy that I am able to message a little with my husband. I have been pretty lucky to get a hold of him and have service sporadically throughout the day.

CHAPTER 20

July 16 - 6:01 a.m.

38.2 miles / 7,372 feet

15 hours, 27 minutes

"Set goals, challenge yourself, and achieve them.
Live a healthy life... and make every moment count.
Rise above the obstacles, and focus on the positive."
-Robert Goddard

I AWAKE WITH A DETERMINATION to change my approach today. I have been hiking so late into the evenings, thus making it difficult for me to get up in the mornings. Today, I will work hard to camp no later than nine-thirty and be fast asleep by ten. If I can get up earlier, it will allow me time to use more daylight.

I also make a goal of checking off one of my bucket list items: "Eat a large package of Oreos." Out of all my food, the Oreos weigh the most and take up precious room in my pack. I grab the Ziploc bag of delicious cookies and place half of the Oreos into my front hip belt pocket. For easy access, I put the remaining cookies in the side mesh of my pack with the rest of today's food. I grab a handful of Oreos for breakfast, washing them down with my chocolate Silverstar nutrition protein. It is a chocolate overload, and I love it!

My body also finally decides it does not need all the extra fluid it has been storing. Since the start of my morning, I have begun to pee every thirty minutes, decreasing the swelling in my feet. However, they have not reduced enough to take away the pain I feel in my heel. I stop a few times to figure out what is causing the pain, and I soon realize that the back part of my shoe is pushing against my swollen and blistered heel. To minimize the pain, I use my tiny Swiss army knife's scissors and cut off the top part of my shoe and some of the lower padding.

As I fix my shoe with more Oreos stuffed in my mouth, something purple catches the corner of my eye. I take a moment to focus on the object until I can figure out what it is. I soon realize that it is a purple balloon. The balloon managed to make its way up here and has settled onto a tree stump. Other colors quickly trigger your sight when all you see are the shades of greens and blues of nature. I shift my gaze back to my heel before I stand up and move my foot around, hoping that I have fixed the problem. I take a few steps and there is no more pain.

Soon after I reach the 300-mile mark, I notice rocks laced with the color of turquoise all over the trail—what a fascinating place to mark this milestone. I reach down to pick one up, and it crumbles in my hand instantly. I hike up a little further until I see one I know won't turn to dust. I reach down and pick it up, admiring its beauty, snap a photo, and return it to the way it was. When I have phone service, I will send a picture to my brother. He is good at identifying minerals. When he responds, I learn they are mica crystals.

The trail then leads me to the Mike Urich Cabin. I had hoped to make it here last night but came nowhere close. It is the first cabin the PCT crosses heading southbound. I don't miss the opportunity to enter and take a look around. Inside, there's a table, a bench, and a large wood stove. There's even a pack of cards and some poker chips. It is pretty big inside with plenty of space for people to set up for the night so long as they don't mind the company of mice. Once I leave the cabin, I stop at the stream not too far away. I chug the remaining water I have and refill two water bottles this time. From here, it is only five miles to my next water source and an additional eight-mile hike until I reach a piped spring. The piped spring provides me with icy cold, delicious water. Probably the best tasting water I have had all day.

I soon enter another burned field filled with wild lupine flowers that stand out amidst all the burned-up trees and help bring the area back to life. With several long deep breaths, I take in the sweet smell of these stunning purple flowers. I am surprised at the sheer number of them and realize that I have enjoyed everything the trail has offered me today, as well as being able to stuff my face with more cookies. Although I climb several mountains, they are not too technical or long. Most are above the clouds, which are moving at a much faster pace than I am. I even manage to get service near the Basin Trail Junction.

I find a fantastic spot at Sheep Lake to camp for the night. It is not too far from the highway, so most tent sites are taken up by weekenders. Since I set my tent up right next to the lake, I wash my feet before going to bed and stand in the water for a bit, letting the ice-cold water ease the pain in my sore and achy feet while finishing up the last of my Oreos.

I thought by now I would be sick of Oreos, but I am not. I could easily do this challenge all over again tomorrow. The thought of jumping in the lake to check off another bucket list item crosses my mind, but I am too tired, and the water is freezing. Instead, I return to my tent, feeling accomplished, feet refreshed, and happy I have lessened the weight of my pack. As I lay there snuggled inside my quilt, I take a look at the map on my phone. Excitement fills my mind as I learn where tomorrow will bring me.

CHAPTER 21

DAY 14 FKT ATTEMPT

July 17 - 6:03 a.m.

35.3 miles / 5,469 feet

14 hours, 44 minutes

"Even the smallest act of caring for another person is like a drop of water; it will make ripples throughout the entire pond."

-Bryan Matteo

AFTER LOOKING AT THE ROUTE on my map for the second time since last night, I make two small goals for the day. Number one, make it to the privy within the next hour. Number two, make it to the White Pass Kracker Barrel store before it closes. Although my hips are sore from my pack and my feet continue to throb, the start of my day is amazing. I had a great night's sleep next to Sheep Lake. Less than a mile from leaving the campsite, I find myself once again above the clouds. As though Heaven has opened up, the sun quickly makes an appearance, kissing the land with its rays. When the clouds block the sun and the rays have disappeared, gloominess and rain set in. Luckily, I already have my rain jacket on. It is a crisp morning.

When I reach the privies in just thirty minutes, I do a mental celebratory dance. But my celebration quickly comes to an end. The privies are closed for the season because of COVID-19. I make a beeline for the woods. When I return, I take the bridge nearby the rest area and hike over Highway 410 near Chinook Pass, where snow awaits. However, I don't see very many hikers. However, this being a popular trail means people have created several paths in the snow. I check my Guthook guide once again to make sure I am heading in the correct direction, which leads me up toward the top of a snow mound. After trying to hike atop it, I decide it would be safer to follow the path just below and alongside where the trail should be. I sit down on the snow and joyfully slide thirty feet below on my bottom until I am at the base. I continue to hike in and out of snow. Roughly ten miles later, I reach Mount Rainier National Park. Since the trail hugs its border, I spend the next several miles crossing into and out of the park.

Determined to make it to the White Pass Kracker Barrel store, I dream of a warm meal, a bottle of soda, and copious amounts of snacks at my disposal. This encourages me to challenge myself just a little harder today. I run all the downs and hike the ups moving faster than usual.

Five miles from the store, the mosquitos come out to play. I grab my mosquito net, placing it over my cap and down my face for protection. They land all over me even though my clothes had been sprayed with permethrin before starting the

PCT. Some still manage to bite me on my shoulders through my shirt. These mosquitos are relentless. I place gloves over my hands and put my rain jacket back on to prevent their vicious bites.

The store is a half-mile off the trail, which adds an extra mile to today's total. I make it to the store with thirty minutes to spare. I turn my phone off airplane mode and am happy to learn I have service. I remove my pack, placing it just outside the door. I reach inside my left pant pocket for my facemask, lather my hands up with sanitizer, and enter the store. The extra half-mile to reach the store is all worthwhile; I meet a welcoming cashier. Being extremely kind, she offers me a place to set up my tent in the back, do laundry, and take a shower. Having more hours of light left to hike, I kindly decline but ask if I may use the restroom. The warm water from the faucet in the bathroom feels incredible. I wash the filth from my face and scrub my hands with vigor. When I return to the store, the cashier lets me stay and eat inside the warmth of the building even though there are only twenty minutes left before closing time.

I end up buying a bean burrito, a piece of chocolate cake, and a soda.

I take a seat at the table closest to the door. As I lean over to grab my piece of chocolate cake, I accidentally tip my soda over, spilling it all over myself, the table, and the floor.

I turn to the cashier. "I am so sorry. Do you have a mop I can use?"

She responds, "Don't worry about it; I will get it. Accidents happen."

Once I finish with dinner, I return to the shelves, picking out additional snacks: a bag of jerky, a muffin, chips, and gummies. As I am getting ready to leave, the cashier stops me.

"Do you want any of the remaining food here? It is all the unsold warm food from today," she offers.

I respond with an excited, "Yes!"

She tells me I can take it all if I want. I can't resist the offer and happily say, "Yes, please," again. She grabs a paper bag and carefully places burritos, corn dogs, breakfast sandwiches, a ham and cheese sandwich, and a large sausage into it. As I exit the store, I thank her for her kindness and tell her that I will share the food with any hikers I come across.

I take out a corn dog and sausage before opening my pack and stuffing the paper bag full of goodies inside. As I wield my backpack onto my shoulders, I feel the food's weight instantly. It brings me back to my high school days of carrying large textbooks in my backpack.

I still have service, so I begin to message my husband. I tell him about the lady's kindness from the store and how I had to push myself extra hard to get there in time. I am tired and ready to sleep for the night. He urges me to get some rest and start early in the morning.

I take a look at my map and pick out a new campsite location a few miles ahead. It is the only water source for nine miles. I make the slow and steady climb towards it. Once I reach the area, my heart drops. Two hikers have already claimed the site and set up for the night. It is eight-thirty, and I am ready for bed. I just want to curl up into a ball and sleep. I am exhausted, and all that food I had eaten has turned me into a sleepy zombie. Thankfully, the hikers call me over and say there is enough room to set up my tent. It is the first time since leaving my family near Hart's Pass that I have had to share a campsite with someone.

I learn my neighbors are father and son. They are section hiking, heading northbound towards Stevens Pass. Since they are heading where I had just come from, and I am heading where they are going, we share intel about trail conditions. I am sad to learn that I will need to use my dreaded crampons for the next few days. As I talk with them, I notice that they have their dinner set aside, a dehydrated meal. I then tell them about the kindness of the lady from the Kracker Barrel store. I grab the paper bag of food out of my backpack and choose a few items I will want to eat tomorrow. I ask the men if they would like any. They respond with, "Yes—Heck yes!" I tell them I already grabbed what I wanted from the bag, and they can have the rest.

As I lay in bed that night tossing and turning, I hear them talking. The father tells his son about trail magic. His son responds, "What's that?" The father explains that trail magic is an act of kindness towards hikers. Sometimes people will set aside food in coolers next to the trail specifically for hikers. He then tells him that you usually get trail magic from other people, but it's very rare that you get it from a backpacker. This makes me smile.

I continue moving around a lot on my sleeping pad, feeling guilty for making so much noise. My legs are restless and achy, and my feet throb with pain. I put my pack under them and try to elevate them while sleeping on my side. I am unable to stay still. Then, just as I begin to doze off, I awake to a loud but recognizable noise.

CHAPTER 22

"Of all the fire mountains, which like beacons once blazed along the Pacific Coast, Mount Rainier is the noblest."
-John Muir

BY FIVE-THIRTY, I am wide awake. I did not sleep well at all. One of the men sleeping in the tent next to me woke me several times throughout the night, making me wish I had a pair of ear-plugs to block out the excessive snoring. I lie in bed a few more minutes before deciding to get up and get going. I pack up as quietly as possible as not to wake my neighbors.

A ton of mosquitos swarm around this morning, forcing me to put on my head net and gloves. The number of mosquitos landing and buzzing on my head net and next to my ears is enough to drive a person mad. I swat at them in vain but eventually give up. It is just wasted energy. The real problem is going to the bathroom. I really have to go, but I don't want a bottom full of bites. I hold it in, hoping to make it to an area free and clear of these beasts.

I finally reach the Devil's Thumb rock formation. Giving me a thumbs up, the spot is easy to identify with its rocky peak sticking out higher than the rest of the mountain. The hikers last night warned me about this area. As they had suggested, crampons or microspikes are needed to cross through the snow. To make it safely across, I will need to use the steps embedded in the snow by previous hikers. There are no trees in this section and nothing to grab or catch if I slip.

Before reaching into my pack for my microspikes, I take one long look at my hands. They appear as though they are not my own, covered in grime and bruises. Although I do my best to wash them throughout my days, they still look so filthy. Spending weeks in the snow and not using gloves to get a better grip on my ice axe has stained them with dark purple and black colors. My hands have become scabbed, worn, and weathered, as though they have aged twenty years. I send a picture of them to my husband. He responds back that they look slightly frostbitten. Luckily, it is nothing major, and the discoloration should go away within a few weeks.

I sit and soak in the view, putting on my microspikes slowly. Like the mountains I have hiked previously, the beauty of looking out is enough to take your breath away and bring a tear to your eye. Mountains upon mountains and trees upon trees with a lake far off in the distance make me feel like I am on top of the world. I am suddenly met with a rush of gratitude. Thankful for all the support I have been given along my journey, I say a quick prayer. I pray for those who have been praying for me. I pray for those who may need prayer. I thank the creator for giving me these views, and I thank all those who have helped me along my journey. I say my Indian name aloud, "Isht' Putaki, Flys High Woman."

I continue hiking but find it difficult to concentrate on the task at hand with a view like this. After a few steps, the rubber on my microspike digs into my left heel and big toe, emitting measurable pain. I stop and take another seat and take off the microspikes, replacing them with the crampons. This fixes the problem instantly, and I can continue only stopping every few steps to take in the view.

Once I reach the other side of the Devil's Thumb, I'm back in the tree line. The views from here are just as remarkable, and I now have a clear view of Mount Rainier in the distance. Finally, I notice a less sizable amount of mosquitos up here. I quickly find a tree and am able to use the restroom comfortably.

I finally make my way to the Goat Rocks Knife's Edge Traverse, whose name gives this portion of the trail some solid justice. Several hikers are out today, and I soon learn why. The views are even more spectacular than before, and I am well above the tree line now.

Looking at what I am about to cross reminds me of a dream I've had many times before. In my dream, I am scaling mountain peaks. I skip atop each peak as though I am floating across their ridges. In reality, hiking my way across the Knife's Edge marks a remarkable realization that I am living this dream. The vast amount of cascade peaks and volcanoes seen from here gives off immense power. I feel a certain strength come over me as though I am feeding off the mountain's energy. *Wow*, I cannot believe what I am doing. Had this been earlier in my hike, this would have shaken me to my core. I have come a long way since.

This trail section definitely tests me with its sketchy, sheer drop-offs on each side. In some areas, there is barely room to cross. Luckily, I don't cross paths with anyone hiking northbound. Making it further ahead on the trail, I am no longer hiking atop a ridge. Instead, I am hiking just below and to the right of it. To one side, the security of the mountain. To the other, another drop-off.

I eventually reach a fork on the trail. I can either take the alternate high route or follow the path exactly and hike the snowy Pacific Crest Trail route. The safest option will be to take the high course. Knowing I cannot take any alternate routes, I look at the trail ahead to determine if it seems safe before making any decisions. There are tracks in the snow that seem to be a few days old. The area also looks less technical than what I have already experienced. I make up my mind that I will just go for it. I take a seat to put my crampons on once again and grab my ice axe from my pack.

I slowly traverse my way across, embedding new prints in the snow. My confidence in my equipment and my ability to traverse snow has grown. Had this been earlier in my journey, I am almost sure I'd have taken the high route. It is slow going as I take my time crossing. Another hiker soon catches up. He is only wearing microspikes and is sinking his feet into my steps along the way. We soon reach a snowless rock. I take a seat to tell him he can go around me since he is moving faster. He then takes two steps and slips, barely catching himself from falling. He takes two steps back towards me, reaches into his pack for his ice axe, and says, "That's okay, I will just follow you." When we finally reach the other side, he tells me he should have just taken the high route, and we both laugh.

I trudge along and slowly but surely finish this section. I am amazed at the number of hikers and the number of tents already set up for the night. At this campsite, hikers can see Mount Rainier, Mount St. Helens, and Mount Adams in one setting like nowhere I have been on the PCT. I can only imagine what a sunset and sunrise looks like from here. I still have hours left in my day to hike. I tell myself that one day I will come back and camp here with my family.

Making the descent from this point is gorgeous. The trail eventually leads to another water crossing with no way around but to walk through the Cyprus River. To the left of the crossing is a beautiful waterfall. I stay standing in the water for an extra minute to alleviate my achy feet. I reach down and scoop up some water, refilling my bottles and washing my face.

Once I am well away from the waterfall, I take another look at my phone. Today's snow has slowed me down once again. I begin to devise a new plan. I will camp at mile 392 next to a small stream. I decide I won't be boiling any water for a hot meal tonight in order to get there in time. Instead, I cold soak my dinner of pasta primavera with the icy cold water I pulled from the waterfall. I wait an hour before eating. When my food has had plenty of time to rehydrate, I reach into my front right pouch for my spork, but I can't find it. I remove every item out of my pouch, searching for my utensil. Still, I see nothing. I look through my left hip belt pouch. Once again, nothing. Without a spork, I turn the Ziploc bag, place the open corner of it next to my mouth, and begin to eat in the same manner as if it were the last chips in a bag.

When I reach my planned mile marker for the night, I sit down to gather water. I am not even seated for a second before I am swarmed by an absurd number of mosquitos. I quickly get up and get moving, putting as much distance away from me and the water as possible. The mosquitos continue to follow until I eventually give up. There will be no mosquito-free campsite tonight. I set up camp and hang my bear bag just a half-mile from the water source. I then throw my pack inside and crawl in as fast as possible. I zip up my tent and use my headlamp and look around for any critters that may have snuck their way in. I can hear more buzzing outside my tent. I have to use the bathroom but don't want to deal with the mosquitos. I will hold it until the morning.

Chapter 23

Day 16 FKT Attempt

July 19 - 6:19 a.m.

39.75 miles / 5,702 feet

15 hours, 23 minutes

"I thought leaving the dead mosquitos on my face might warn off the others, but if anything it just makes them angrier."

-Charlie Knight

THIS MORNING, the annoyance of the vast number of mosquitos helps me quickly pack up. It is a chilly start to my hike, but I warm up after a short climb. I try to eat breakfast, but the number of mosquitos trying to attack me makes it difficult to consume anything. I searched everywhere for my spork this morning, but it is nowhere to be found. I still haven't used the bathroom and have to go badly, but there are so many mosquitos out. It takes a few hours of hiking until I can't hold it any longer. I make it to a less mosquito-infested area but still end up with three bites on my rear end.

When I reach Mount Adams, I take my water bottle out from the side of my pack to filter. As I lean over, the flask connected to my filter falls out of my front pouch, falling into and down a waterfall. "No, no, no," I begin to repeat to myself. Part of me wants to leave it. I have another filter anyway, but what if that filter fails? It takes hours for my iodine tablets to work, and I only brought a few. Thankfully, my water flask catches onto a bit of land just below.

I remove my pack and scramble down towards the flask. It is not a challenging climb down, just tiring and time-consuming. This is the second time my filter has fallen out of my pack and in the most inconvenient places. Once I retrieve it, I remind myself to secure it with the band attached to my bottle holder. When I am back to where my pack sits, I stretch the band out from my water bottle holder and wrap it two times around my plastic foldable drinking flask.

I remove my shoes and roll up my pants while taking in the view of Mount Adams. Growing up in Washington State, I have always seen this mountain in the distance. Being able to hike alongside it is something I had never dreamed of doing. Being this close to the glaciers of this mountain seems surreal, like something from a painting. I wish I could sit a little longer and continue soaking it all in, but the mosquitos have discovered my whereabouts. They begin to bite away at my exposed skin. I quickly roll my pant legs down, put on my socks and shoes, and get the heck out of there.

The temperature has really risen today. I find a patch of snow alongside the trail and brush away the dirt from the top part of it, placing the cleaner snow on my neck to cool down. I then grab another ball of clean snow and begin to munch away. It tastes just like a snow cone, and I can't help myself and grab more. In the back of my mind, I know this isn't the best of decisions. I have no idea how long this snow has been sitting. But it tastes incredible, so I take the risk and help myself to another serving.

I end my evening with a three-mile climb. Just like the night before, this area has an absurd number of mosquitos. The trail looks as if no one has been through here in quite some time. My path is scattered with untouched spider webs. I dodge most of them except the huge one crossing the entire trail. I somehow miss seeing it. The web sticks to my head net, making my skin crawl. I swiftly pull it off of my head, hoping there isn't a spider attached to it. I search my clothes for anything that may be crawling atop of me. I find nothing but am still creeped out at the possibility of hiking into more.

It seems my nights are becoming a routine. Slowly removing my shoes and peeling off my socks, I give my shoes a once over, noticing the holes growing larger and more numerous by the day. My shoes are falling apart. The little parts of my foot that are near the holes catch sand and dirt through these newly made access points. The sand then sticks to my wet feet, creating friction between my socks and skin. In turn, the number of blisters forming on the sides of my feet are causing me to take extra stops to care for them.

Every night, I remove the bandages from my feet and continue to spend at least thirty minutes massaging them. My right heel is extremely swollen today, and my left toe is painful to raise. The throbbing and achiness keep me from falling fast asleep. However, I have noticed that in the past few days, my feet have been getting stronger. They don't seem to start becoming unbearable until I have been hiking for at least twelve hours. Even though I have a high pain threshold, this makes the last few hours of my day torturous.

Nights are wrought with exhaustion. Completely spent by the end of the day, negative thoughts course throughout my mind. My thoughts sometimes keep me from sleeping. I toss and turn, wondering, *Can I do this for the next two months? I'm not even halfway through, or can I even continue to do this?* This defeatist banter wavers back and forth through my mind. It's impossible to answer these questions at night when I am physically and mentally broken down.

Finally, when the night has come to an end and it's a new day, my mind always changes for the better. My attitude improves, I eat some breakfast, and my feet aren't feeling so beat up. The morning and new outlook motivate me to keep going. I focus on staying positive, optimistic, and grateful. I try to set small goals. I look at the map on my phone and see what I'm supposed to be crossing for the day. I focus on what I need to complete today instead of getting overwhelmed with the total mileage of the PCT I have left to finish. Whether it's an actual bathroom, a mountain, a road, somewhere I may have service, or something that sparks interest, I try to stay motivated and remain grateful. Tomorrow, my goal will be the most mileage I've attempted to complete in one day so far.

CHAPTER 24

DAY 17 FKT ATTEMPT

July 20 - 6:14 a.m.

39.8 miles / 4,167 feet

15 hours, 47 minutes

"You have permission to walk away from anything that doesn't feel right. Trust your instincts and listen to your inner-voice-it's trying to protect you."

-Bryant Mcgill

I WAKE UP READY TO HIT THE TRAIL once again and face the spiderwebs. There are so many zig-zagging webs hanging from tree to tree on the trail. After running into one yesterday, I raise my trekking pole and wave it in front of me while walking to prevent any from getting onto my head net. I have a pretty gradual climb to start today, about five miles.

Along with the webs, the mosquitos continue bugging me. Although an annoyance, they keep me moving quickly to avoid them. Every time I try to stop and take a break, they swarm around me. By noon it is hot, and the mosquitos have dissipated and become too tired to feast on me.

Berries lay scattered along the trail, and I don't hesitate to pick any. I feel a rush of energy from their sugars, and as much as I'd like to stay a little longer to gather more, I am all too eager to get in as many miles as I can today. I should reach the Bridge of the Gods by tomorrow.

My left calf begins to feel really tight, causing me to limp. I do what I can to massage it out, but it continues to ache. The achiness comes and goes. I ignore it and push on.

By nine tonight, I am ready to be finished for the day, but I don't make it to a campsite until ten. Once I reach the area, I notice someone camped there already, and the site doesn't look big enough for an additional tent. I look at my map to see my next campsite options. I could hike an extra five miles or hike a quarter of a mile off trail and set up at an actual campground. I end up taking the road and hiking the quarter of a mile to the Panther Creek Campground, mile 470.6.

Although it is late, the camp host is still awake and has a fire going. We greet one another. The young man in his late twenties offers me a chair and a beer. I don't smell that great and am extremely filthy, so I am hesitant to take him up on his offer. He tells me it's okay, and he always offers that chair and a beer to all PCT hikers that pass through. Red flags go off inside my head. A weird feeling fires up in my gut. I can't say exactly what is suspicious, but I don't trust this man. I even doubt that he offers every hiker the same treatment.

The red flags start screaming at me to leave as I take a seat. Especially since I haven't even been seated for thirty seconds before he offers his RV shower to me. He also asks if I am single.

I quickly respond that I am married, have three kids, and no, I would not like a shower. He shifts the conversation quickly, but I am ready to fall asleep and don't really care to visit with him. I then ask him how much it costs to camp there. He tells me I could camp for free so long as I set up on the empty slate near the RV site. The free site is also close to where his RV sits. I ignore my instinct to get the heck out of there and set up near the RV site for the night.

Once again, I find myself tossing and turning, trying to fall asleep, unsure if it's the creepiness of the camp host or the achiness in my legs. I wake up several times throughout the evening to massage my feet. I fall asleep for a few short hours before I am awakened by footsteps outside of my tent.

OREGON

"I went to the woods because I wished to live
deliberately, to front only the essential facts of life,
and see if I could not learn what it had to teach, and not,
when I came to die, discover that I had not lived."

-Henry David Thoreau

CHAPTER 25

DAY 18 FKT ATTEMPT

July 21 - 5:54 a.m.

36 miles / 6,588 feet

15 hours, 12 minutes

"Many a trip continues long after movement
in time and space have ceased."

-John Steinbeck

THE FOOTSTEPS ARE FROM THE CAMP HOST. He is already up and patrolling the area this morning. I quickly pack up my gear to get as far away from the campground as possible. Within ten minutes, I am back on the road heading to where I left off yesterday.

I relook at my Guthook guide for any information someone may have posted about the host at the campground. I try to talk myself out of my experience, but I can't ignore my gut. It would be a few weeks later before someone would write about their experience warning female hikers about the host who is, "...a little too friendly if you are a solo female hiker, consider camping down by the creek." When I find this out, I am disappointed in myself. First, I should have left the area immediately, and number two, I should have also posted about it on the Guthook guide. Even if the man was harmless, I am alone out here and need to be smart about the choices I make.

Although I had a rough night, I am happy to know I only have thirty-five miles left until I reach Bridge of the Gods and cross into Oregon today!

The trail beams green. Giant banana slugs cover everything. They must be over six inches long. I try not to step on any. Flowers run wild, and the smell of sweet grass fills the air. My Aunt Minnie once told me that whenever I smell sweet grass, consider it a blessing. The thought of this makes me smile as I continue to slowly take in every breath.

My last big climb before making the hike down into Oregon is littered with bright yellow flowers. I have never seen so many in one place before. Instantly, I am reminded of my Aunt Brenda. Cancer took her life a few years back. I had not thought of her since starting the PCT, but I feel her walking alongside me for some reason. I feel her cheering me on with her "you got this girl" attitude. I shift my thoughts towards the trail again and begin to think about how much of an emotional roller coaster ride the PCT is turning out to be.

I also know that I should be days ahead of where I am now. I begin to give myself a positive pep talk. As if trying to reassure myself, I say, "This is exactly where I was meant to be. In this place, in this space, and in this time."

As I make my final climb down towards the Bridge of the Gods, I turn my phone off airplane mode and call my Aunt Minnie. Her voice is a much-needed distraction from the pain in my feet. I tell her about my day and about the sweet grass. She laughs as I begin to talk to her with a mouth full of raspberries that are now abundant along the trail.

Once I hang up, I message my sister to let her know I only have a few miles to go. Hiking downhill puts more pressure on my feet. This portion is rocky, and every step feels like I am walking on pins and needles. I block out the pain and shift my thoughts toward my kids. I am all too excited that in less than an hour I get to see them.

As I continue to hike down, I can get a glimpse of what lies ahead until I have finally made it. I've reached the Bridge of the Gods! Located in Cascade Locks, Oregon, it is the lowest elevation point on the entire PCT. The bridge is narrow and shared between pedestrians, vehicles, and cyclists. Since the path taken to walk across has several openings at the bottom with the Columbia River just below, I make sure to tuck away all loose objects. I take my time crossing, enjoying every minute of the bridge. I have already been through so much just to get to this point and would cry if I wasn't already emotionally drained.

When I finally make it to the hotel, my kids and sister are waiting outside for me. As much as they want to hug and kiss me, I smell horrendous. The looks on my children's faces as they make their way towards me agree. I tell them to let me shower first, and then they can hug me all they want.

Before washing up, I sit in the hotel room for a few minutes, talking to my kids. They all give me shocked expressions once I remove my shoes and show off my gnarly blisters. My sister holds nothing back and tells me I smell so bad, and my shoes stink even worse. We both laugh, and I say, "Okay, okay, I will shower." I slowly stand up and wobble my way to the bathroom.

I don't hesitate to look in the mirror this time. I am so skinny. I have been eating more since the Summit Inn. Still, it almost seems worthless compared to the number of calories I am burning throughout the day.

The warm shower feels fantastic. If only I had sent a resupply box here, I could be taking a hot Epsom salt bath tonight. Feeling exhausted, I take a seat, grab a washcloth, and begin to scrub away the filth. I watch the dirt and grime slowly work their way towards the drain. I am gentle with cleaning my tired and blistered feet. I have blisters on my pinky toes that I have been hesitant to pop for fear of infection. Since I can wash my feet, I pop them one by one and watch the liquid ooze its way out.

My Smartwool legging and a bra are all I wear once I exit the bathroom. I put my down jacket on, gather my smelly torn shoes and clothes, and limp my way to the laundry room. I return minutes later. My sister comments on the amount of weight I have lost so far. Never the one to bite her tongue, she tells me like it is. "How much have you been eating, sis? You need to eat more." I nod in agreement.

As I lay in bed that night, I make a social media post about finally getting out of Washington. I don't want people to know exactly where I am on the PCT trail, so I won't post until I am a few more days ahead. I keep my post simple, "Washington, I leave you with frostbitten hands, bruises, scrapes, scabs, and achy tired feet. I'm physically and mentally exhausted. I've tripped and fallen more times than I can count. My pants are torn, my shoes are torn, and I lost my spork. The trails were rough and rugged. The climbs were epic. I am from Wapato, Washington, and it has been an amazing journey through my home state. Now on to Oregon."

CHAPTER 26

DAY 19 FKT ATTEMPT

July 22 - 11:14 a.m.

28.7 miles / 6,955 feet

10 hours, 47 minutes

"Family is not an important thing, it's everything."
-Michael J. Fox

THE COMFORT OF A WARM BED makes it difficult to wake up. My family and I take our time getting ready. The cafe next door is open and only a few steps away from my hotel room. I order biscuits and gravy for breakfast and a slice of cherry pie. I ask the server for a plastic spoon to take with me on the trail.

I finally decide it is time to ditch some of my heavier winter gear. I search my pack and take out everything I won't be needing anymore. I rid myself of my crampons, ice axe, stove, and silk liner. I keep my microspikes just in case. I then make the 0.2-mile hike to the post office to mimic mailing off my items, only I give them to my sister and kids. She thinks it's silly that I didn't give them to her at the hotel, but I tell her it is important I don't shortcut the rules.

We all return back to the hotel at ten-thirty. I purchase a soda from the vending machine before setting off. We don't begin hiking until eleven. My kids ask if they can join me on my first mile. I give them an enthusiastic, "Yes!" and mentally tick off another bucket list item: "Hike with my kids."

On the trail, we take our time enjoying every moment together. We find ourselves stopping every few steps to pick salmonberries and raspberries. We each try an Oregon grape, and our mouths pucker with the tart taste. My kids and I all agree that the other berries taste better.

Besides the act of kindness from the White Pass Kracker Barrel Store, it is here where I have my first official run-in with trail magic. The trail magic appears inside a green and red container labeled in capital letters, "TRAIL MAGIC," followed by, "PCT hikers" with a heart and Lemonade and Pine Needle trail names. When I open it, it is filled with soda. Since I still have a bottle of soda in my pack from this morning, I don't grab any. I slowly close up the container, smile, and tell my kids that someone else may be in greater need. I then explain to them what trail magic means.

When the time finally comes for them to turn back, they don't want to leave. My sister apologizes that she cannot stay any longer because she has to work the night shift and really has to get back. We all kiss and hug each other goodbye. Seeing my kids and sister, and being able to hike with them, gives me an absurd amount of joy and energy. I feel refreshed.

It is over a 5,000-foot hike up from the Bridge of the Gods. By ten that night, I am still full of energy, so I keep going. I feel good and move with ease. The low mileage from today and getting rid of my extra winter gear give my feet a break. They are only slightly aching. By eleven-thirty, I know I should get some sleep and start early in the morning. I pass several campsites already occupied before reaching an empty trail junction.

CHAPTER 27

DAY 20 FKT ATTEMPT

July 23 - 6:29 a.m.

47.1 miles / 7,589 feet

16 hours, 52 minutes

"Technology is a useful servant,
but a dangerous master."

-Christian Louse Lang

THE MORNING LIGHT FROM THE SUNRISE wakes me from my slumber. I check the time: 5:46 a.m. I pull my quilt over my head and attempt to fall back asleep. It's pointless. I don't even know why I tried. I do nothing more than toss and turn. Ten minutes later, I am pulling my hiking shirt over my head, yawning. I stretch my arms out and roll my neck from side to side. My left shoulder feels tight. I begin to massage it, but just like my sleep, it's pointless.

I anxiously look at my phone. I didn't charge it last night, so I try plugging it in again while I get ready and pack up my things. Another ten minutes pass. I pick up my phone, still no additional charge. I unplug it, then plug it back in a few times.

Still, nothing. I wiggle the cord around. Once again, nothing. I scroll down to check the power level: eighty percent. I turn to my Guthook guide as I had the night before, double-checking the distance to my next resupply point. It's almost twenty-two miles away. I turn my phone to the dimmest setting just in case and stuff my phone into my pants pocket. I do not want a repeat of what happened to me in Washington. If my power banks and phone run out of power, it will be nearly impossible to find my way. Although I am glad there isn't an absurd amount of snow here, the possibility of losing power to one of my most essential resources makes me feel uneasy.

I have biscuits and gravy for breakfast, but the plastic spoon I got a few days prior also snaps in half. Despite the mishap with my spoon and phone, my morning sails by flawlessly otherwise. The sun shines brightly, providing just the right amount of warmth.

By noon, I know I am getting close to the Timberline Lodge, where my resupply awaits. Several day hikers are out and about, making me feel like I have the plague. Being out in nature has made me forget about COVID-19. I am quickly reminded as I begin to pass each day hiker. They all pull up their face masks or step off the trail well away from me. I put my neck gaiter on and begin to act in the same manner. Every time I come within six feet of anyone, I place it over my mouth and nose. Once I am past them, I pull it back down, taking deep breaths as though I am gasping for air.

By noon, I have made my way to the Lodge with Mount Hood, watching my every move. The mountain looks like nothing more than a giant slab of rock sprinkled with snow. Considering how bare the mountain seems, I am shocked at how many skiers and snowboarders are there. As I enter the lodge, I place my pack on a chair near the dining facility. Each table is evenly spaced apart, and only every other table is open for seating. I open my pack and pull out my electronics bag. I take one long look at my watch before removing it to charge. I realize I have set a new PCT personal record. It has taken me seven hours to hike twenty-one miles and climb 5,500 feet.

I plug my phone in, and just like before, nothing happens. I stuff it back into my pocket, and grab the rest of my electronics and plug them in. I walk down the stairs using the rail for support. It feels so awkward to walk without anything weighing down on my shoulders. I feel so light, and my posture seems to have improved. I am not hunching forward like I usually do.

There are several little shops downstairs. I hope that one of them has a new iPhone cord. As I approach the cashier from the first shop I see, I feel awkward when asking for an iPhone cord. I look like a hot mess, don't smell great, and besides my family, I haven't had an actual face-to-face conversation with anyone in quite some time. After speaking with the cashier, she tells me I am in luck because they have one left. I take a deep breath mustering a, "Thank goodness," as I exhale. I really can't believe it only cost me five dollars. Once I leave the shop, I find the resupply location. I am charged a ten-dollar holding fee, but I don't mind because what's inside is well worth the cost.

The walk back and up the stairs turns out even slower as I begin to wince in pain. I use the rail to help ease my way up. As usual, my feet have been hurting all day. I reach the tables next to the dining facility and set my box down. I then make my way towards the wonderful smell of food.

Unlike when I first arrived, the doors to the dining facility are now shut. The sign on the door says that they close at two. I look at the time; it is 2:01. The doors are not locked, so I go ahead and go in since no one tells me otherwise. I grab a few food and drink items then head to the sandwich bar. I am the last person in line. I order a turkey sandwich with lettuce, tomato, cheese, and pickles.

When I get back to my table, I kick off my battered shoes and elevate my feet on the chair across from me. I devour the entire turkey sandwich; gone within minutes. My ice cream sandwich doesn't last long either. I wash everything down with a bottle of orange mango juice, soda, and half of an icy cold latte, but save the other half for later. I ate and drank so much; my stomach feels like it is about to burst.

I tear open my resupply box in excitement. I have been waiting for this moment for over 200 miles. As I open the box, my brand new, clean, and fresh-smelling, non-torn shoes catch my eyes first. In reality, I should have tossed my trail runners after 300 miles. The amount of pain they have caused me for the past few weeks is soon forgotten as I look down at my new shoes. I envision a bright light radiating from them while raising them high up into the air. The scene where the king holds up the newly knighted prince in the movie *The Lion King* crosses my mind. My shoe gaiters are tucked inside. The gaiters help prevent rocks and dirt from getting inside the shoes. I don't know what my reason was for waiting until now to have them.

Under my shoes sits my cut-down sleeping mat. I am over having to air up my sleeping pad each night. Having a sleeping mat will save me some time and effort, especially after long days.

I look at the rest of my items. I have no idea how I managed to stuff all of my resupply food inside. Since my spoon broke earlier, I don't remove the spoons attached to my tuna packets. Even though they are small, they are better than nothing. It feels great to have more food, but it is a little disappointing in the amount of weight I will be adding to my pack.

I take out my bear bag and begin to stuff it with my food, very Tetris-like. I message my husband as I am packing everything up. I have to admit, I miss the sound of his voice. We have only been able to message back and forth. I then call my mother and talk with all of my kids. When I am finished, I message my friend Rebecca to post social media updates.

My eyes become heavy after all the food eaten, so I allow myself a few minutes to rest. I desperately want to take a nap or sleep for days. Instead, I pack my resupply and head out the door. I am blessed with a four-mile descent. My new shoes feel as if I am walking on clouds, and my feet applaud every step.

I still have a few bars of service. I call my friends Jordan and Lymaris. They, too, are married to active-duty soldiers. Our husbands introduced us during ultra-marathons a few years ago. I met Jordan while running the Coldwater Rumble 100-mile ultra marathon in 2016 and met Lymaris later in the year at the Franklin Mountain half marathon trail race. We were all stationed in El Paso, Texas, together, enjoyed running, and just so happen to be similar in age. Our families were soon running, hiking, and camping together. We often took turns racing. The husbands would race while we watched the kids, and the following week would be our turn. Jordan and Lymaris understand my passion for long treks. Their support and ear lending have played an influential role in my Pacific Crest Trail preparation.

I have not spoken with them in over a month. It is so good to hear the excitement in their voices as I tell them a little about my journey. I eventually start to feel nauseous but chalk it up to all the food and drinks I just consumed. After a few more minutes of talking, the signal becomes weak, making it difficult to hear one another. They give me words of encouragement until I can no longer hear them. I have lost all bars of service on my phone. I turn it back to airplane mode and continue walking another mile. But I suddenly stop, as everything I had eaten begins to make its way to the roof of my mouth. I take a few steps off the trail before I find myself hunched over, throwing up. I immediately feel better and resume the same pace I had been hiking earlier in the day.

My morning goal of fifty miles soon fades as I reach mile forty. Once again, I don't want to take ownership for missing my goal. It's difficult for me to admit failure. Instead, I blame everything from throwing up to stopping for resupply and waiting for my electronics to charge.

CHAPTER 28

DAY 21 FKT ATTEMPT

July 24 - 6:02 a.m.

44.7 miles / 7,257 feet

16 hours, 33 minutes

"Keep listening to your body.
It'll tell you when something's not okay."

-Emily Infeld

I WAKE UP FEELING A LITTLE NAUSEOUS AGAIN. After eating breakfast and drinking a cup of warm PERC Coffee, I start feeling better. Although still nauseous, I continue pushing myself a little harder today. The weather is a little warm but breezy and shady. Several trees lean up against one another, creating a squeaky musical ensemble throughout the woods.

By one-thirty, I make it to Olallie Lake and Resort. I look at my watch and see I have tackled twenty miles in about seven and a half hours. I decide I have earned some extra time to make a stop at the resort's tiny store, a short hike off the trail.

I take my pack off and set it on the bench next to the lake. Sweat covers the back of my shirt and dirt cakes my face. I take

170

out one of my water bottles to clean it off, trying to look somewhat presentable. I am just glad a face mask is required to enter the store so no one can smell my breath. The store has a limited supply of food. I buy a Snickers bar, a bag of chips, and an ice-cold soda before returning to my pack.

I begin eating my snacks and lunch, enjoying the view of Olallie Lake and Mount Jefferson in the distance, where I'll be hiking near today. Knowing it is the second-highest mountain in Oregon makes it look a little intimidating. I can't see the snow conditions, but it seems to be minimal from where I am sitting. According to my Guthook guide, Mount Jefferson is about twenty miles away, so I should be able to camp near it tonight. I place my phone back in my pocket, put my hiking pack back on, and make the short hike back to the start of the trailhead. Ten minutes pass since eating lunch, and I begin to feel even more nauseous than before.

Although I'm feeling sick, my pace hasn't slowed, and it doesn't take me long to hike the easy trail to Milk Creek. From here, it is a long ten-mile climb with over 2,000 feet of vertical gain. Just as predicted, the trail becomes patchy with snow the closer I make it to the top. I wear my microspikes and pass two weekend hikers and their dog.

When I reach the top, the empowering view of Mount Jefferson grips me. For a brief moment, my thoughts of feeling sick disappear as I fixate on the features that make up this volcano. The tree line vanishes at its base, and there is even more snow towards its peak. I am grateful for the trail skirts around it. I'd love to sit a little longer, but it is windy and chilly at the top.

I take a swig of water and take out a packet of crackers to munch. I sweated so much climbing up that my body has already begun to cool off as I sit there. I start to shiver from the wind. I put my raincoat and neck gaiter on to protect myself from the cold. I look back at the hikers making their way towards me. The competitiveness in me doesn't want them to catch up. I take off running and then slow to a walk feeling even worse than before. I begin to yell inside my head, *This section is easy; you should be running! Why are you walking?*

Suddenly, I feel all my energy instantly zap away. I feel deathly ill. I can hardly manage any hiking at all. I'm walking so slowly a slug could beat me at the pace I am going. After another mile, I call it quits for the evening.

I choose a new campsite, only three miles ahead, for the night. But when I reach it, I am disappointed that someone has already claimed the camp there. I hike to the following camp location, but it's taken as well. I try to keep going. The sun begins setting, and darkness soon fades in. Moving at only one mile for every forty-five minutes, I know I need to make it to camp soon. I need to lie down and rest. I feel heated, exhausted, and weak.

I reach the fast-flowing Russell Creek at mile 620.8. Hiking this late into the night only seems to magnify the size of the creek. With my headlamp on, I look up and down the water crossing, searching for a safe passage. Finally, I spot a small rickety bridge someone has made with a few pieces of thin logs. *Thank you, fellow hikers,* I say to myself.

Once I am on the other side of the stream, I shine my headlamp 360 degrees around me. Dead trees cover this side. It is a massive burn area. These damaged trees can fall over at any time, making it an unsafe place to camp. I take out my guide once again to search for the nearest campsite.

The application has the next campsite located two miles ahead at mile 622.5. Notes in the guide from a few hikers say that it is still in a burn area. When I reach the campsite, I take a look around once again. Although sick, I don't feel comfortable with the amount of upright dead trees surrounding me, so I push on. I am moving even slower than before. I haven't eaten dinner. The thought of food makes my stomach turn. I tell myself that I need to make it to camp and will feel better in the morning.

I hike a little longer until I reach the next campsite. I am all out of energy, heated, and sickness has gotten the best of me. I end up setting up camp here for the night. It's the perfect campsite, large and flat, but when I try putting my tent stake in the ground, the stake bounces back. The ground is too hard to plant a tent stake. I use a few rocks to help secure the corners of my tent. The dirt is also so fine that when I'm setting up my tent, every step I take brings up an absurd amount of dust. Someone in the Guthook app commented that it reminds them of a huge ash trash.

It is just past eleven in the evening before I finally make it inside my tent. I don't bother getting into my sleep clothes, and I don't care if this ashtray has covered me in dust. Instead, I set up my sleeping mat and quilt and slowly ease my way inside. I close my eyes to fall asleep but find myself shivering uncontrollably. I am so cold. I know I have a fever. The amount of pain I also feel in my feet has only intensified with how sick I feel. As though someone is punching the life out of my feet and sucking the life out of me, I toss, and I turn, rolling around in hopes everything will magically disappear.

I have just two Tylenol left inside my pack. Do I take them both? If I do, I will need to eat something, which is the last thing on my mind. An hour passes, and I am still shaking. I didn't even hang my bear bag away from camp this evening. I reach inside my bag and pull out one peanut butter cracker, and slowly munch away. I take one Tylenol and one anti-nausea pill. The Tylenol is only half of the dosage I should be taking because I may need the other half tomorrow. I hate taking medicine. Rhabdomyolysis crosses my mind again, and I force myself to drink just a little more water. Another hour passes, my clothes become soaked with sweat. My fever soon breaks as I begin to doze off.

CHAPTER 29

DAY 22 FKT ATTEMPT

July 25 - 8:38 a.m.

22.5 miles / 4,469 feet

10 hours, 53 minutes

"Those memories are stuck in there
and they will come to surface."

-Chris May

WHEN I WAKE UP, I don't want to move. As though I'm resting in a trance, all I find myself doing is staring at the tent's mesh. I lay there for thirty minutes, not wanting to get up, even though I know I should have been gone over an hour ago. It is almost seven-thirty. I finally decide to sit up, but I still don't feel well. I feel nauseous and weak. I have no energy. I begin to beat myself up for not leaving sooner. *Hours wasted are miles lost*, I tell my-self. I don't have time to be sick. I take my time packing up my tent and all additional camp items. I don't leave camp until eight-thirty. I only have a packet of oatmeal for breakfast. It is all I can stomach. I do my best to eat throughout the day but find myself only nibbling away at very little food. The thought of a dehydrated meal makes me feel even sicker. I take another anti-nausea pill. I have three pills left.

I know I won't meet my daily mileage goal, so I devise a new plan. There is a resort seventy-seven miles away. If I can make it there by tomorrow, I can take a shower and get some much-needed rest. Maybe by then, I will have a craving for a solid meal. As the day drags on, so do my feet. I find myself resting every few miles. As though dueling with one another, my mind and body begin to battle. My mind wants to go faster, but my body does not. By afternoon, it is all the same to me. Walk two miles, sit on a rock, mentally beat myself up for stopping, and then continue on the next two miles.

Already feeling down about how slowly I am moving and how sick I am feeling, negativity soon takes over, and flashbacks start. Up until today, I have done an amazing job not thinking much about them. I try to shift my focus on all the beauty that surrounds me, but I keep circling back to my deployment to Iraq. Emotionally and mentally exhausted, I finally give in. For the first time, I begin to allow myself to process the memory fully. Instead of stopping where I drop off the Specialist, I start to think about the outcome and result. Before now, I had never thought about what happened after; I only focused on the negative.

As though it is a puzzle, I put the pieces together and allow myself to feel every emotion. Although it is not the distraction I want from how sick I feel, I don't have the energy to fixate on anything else. My mind has already lost at ignoring the past, and all I can think about is the day our convoy was hit with daisy chain Improvised Explosive Devices. It was the day that left me mentally scarred. Something that was out of my control with an overwhelming feeling of helplessness. Someone's life was in my hands, and I hated it. I knew this man. He was a friend. He was a soldier. He was part of our team. Maybe if he were a stranger, it would have been different. I would be different. There would be no horror movie on repeat inside my head, just a faint memory. I had never felt so helpless as he lay there convulsing. I wanted someone to be there, to help me help him. But instead, I was the medical expert with his life in my hands. It was horrific. I hated seeing him struggle to live. I hated having to give him CPR. I hated that he lost consciousness. I hated the constant questioning of what I could have done better. I hated it, I hated it, I hated it. The drive to the nearest base was minutes away but felt like a lifetime. Like someone had flipped a switch and caused it to slow down. I searched his body up and down for wounds. There were none. His wounds were internal. I yelled and yelled but knew he could not hear me. Sternum rubs did nothing. I felt for a pulse, and it was faint and soon non-existent. But what could I do?

"How much longer to the forward operating base!?" I yelled to my convoy commander. He told me seven minutes. *Dear God, please do not let me lose him,* I thought as I began mouth-to-mouth resuscitation. Praying and breathing for him. His body started to convulse, and once more, I yelled, "HOW MUCH LONGER!?"

"We are almost there!" the convoy commander yelled. Moments later, we were in front of the emergency room. The medics and doctor ran out to help grab his litter. I entered the emergency room, holding one side of the litter. The doctor said they will take care of everything from this point. I stood off to the side, staring, waiting, and praying, watching them work their magic. They intubated him, and from there, things become fuzzy again. I am unable to remember what they did next, only that they called for a Medevac.

Once the Specialist was evacuated by helicopter, I took a sigh of relief. I exited the building, walked over to a cement block, and sat. Just then, a medic and friend I had gone through training with approached me. She had been there from the moment we arrived. I knew she was deployed but didn't know where. We had lost touch since the start of our deployment. She gave me a big hug and told me I had saved his life. Although I felt like I hadn't done much, I thanked my friend for her comforting words, and we hugged each other again as the rest of my team showed back up. Next, I re-entered the Humvee. We left the forward operating base and continued with our mission. I would later find out if we waited for the Medevac to show up near the blast site, it would have taken them over thirty minutes to arrive on the scene, which would have been several minutes too late.

Once our convoy returned to Tallil, Iraq, we were all forced to sit in a circle with a chaplain and talk through what had happened on our mission. Grown men sat there crying, trying to explain their part in the mission. It was a real struggle to sit and listen to everyone. When it got to my turn to say what I had seen and done, I froze. All I could do was look towards the ground and stare at my feet. I could not get any words out. Tears slowly crept down my cheek, and I couldn't talk. I didn't want to talk. Another soldier who I had treated during an earlier mission from an IED blast was sitting next to me. He patted me on the shoulder and said, "It's okay, doc. You don't have to say anything."

After the meeting with the chaplain, I took the long way back to the company. I sat on the steps in front of my room, trying to process everything. One of our squad leaders from the company approached me. He was checking up on me, making sure I was okay. I couldn't bring myself to share what happened. I guess at the time, I was working on burying everything down, and trying to forget it and move on. He said he wished he could take the place of all of his soldiers experiencing bad missions. He sat with me for a few minutes, and we shifted our conversation to what we thought of other bases we had convoyed to. We agreed that Baghdad had the best food.

Later in the evening, as I headed to the chow hall, another Sergeant approached me, asking if I was okay. I found out from him that our convoy commander had left our communications on letting all those near us hear our entire conversation and my pleas for this Specialist to wake. He had heard everything. He also asked if I needed anything. I told both Sergeants I was okay and buried my emotions like I usually had. Unfortunately, years later, those two Sergeants would also suffer from PTSD and commit suicide. One of them occurred only a few weeks before my start of this PCT hike.

A rush of tears coats my cheeks. I know I suffer from PTSD, and it is only now that I am genuinely admitting it to myself and accepting it. I also realize that a part of me enjoys hiking and pushing my body to its limits because I simply can. I am not helpless when I am running and hiking. It is me who is pushing my body forward. I am in control. I don't want to take my life for granted. There may be darkness in the world, but there is also a lot of beauty. The trail continues to prove this over and over again. Maybe this is why I am stuck with this flashback. I am sick, and I can't snap out of it. It is out of my control. What's in my control is where I go from here. I run this entire scenario throughout my mind for several hours until the heat snaps me away from my thoughts.

The sun radiates heat off the rocks and directly towards me. No shade exists to hide under in this huge burn area. I am already overheated, so this can't be good. I take another seat, this time on a hot boulder. I have two full bottles of water left and will need to find a water source soon, so I begin to walk after my short break. I pass a few green and muddy ponds before finally deciding on one to filter water. The top of the water has green algae. I brush it away while submerging my water bottle into the pond. *Yuck!* It tastes horrible and smells even worse. I force myself to drink half of the bottle and pour the other half over my heated face, neck, and head. I refill an additional three water bottles before getting back up to continue hiking.

By evening, I have only gone twenty miles. This distance doesn't cover even half of what I had hiked just yesterday. I am near the Three Fingered Jack. It is one of the oldest high volcanoes in the Cascades Range and looks as frail as me. Erosion has taken its toll. The colorful layering of reds and browns makes it a captivating sight to see.

I find myself again wanting to stop and camp for the night directly where I am standing. Unfortunately, I know a solid climb lies ahead of me, one that brings me closer to Three Fingered Jack. Once I reach the top of this climb, I will be blessed with a nice, long descent. I know I must continue. I need to make it to the top because I may not have the energy for it tomorrow. I slowly drag my feet and give what little power I have left to keep moving forward. I stop every few steps to catch my breath until I finally reach the top. I take a seat to regroup and take in the view. I need all the help I can get. I begin to pray. I pray for strength and energy. I pray for protection. I pray for those who continue to pray for me and those needing prayer. After a few minutes, I know it is time to start moving again. It's only eight-thirty, and there is still some light left in the day. I need to rest. I find the nearest campsite, not too far from the top of this climb. A camper has already set up their tent a few feet away. Thankfully, several campsites are still available in the area, so I take the one closest to the trail.

Before settling into my sleeping quilt, I put on all the warm layers I own. My down jacket is no match for how cold I am. I can't stop shivering. I still have one Tylenol left but may need it in the morning. I take it out of the Ziploc bag and roll it around my fingertips, trying to decide whether to take it or not. I can't do it. Finally, I decide to wait it out since I may need it tomorrow. I slowly place it back into the Ziploc bag and pull out an anti-nausea pill. After this pill, I will only have two left. The drug doesn't seem to do much. I think I am too far gone.

The night drags on. I am so cold, and I can't get comfortable. My stomach begins to hurt as sharp pains course throughout my body. I have to go to the bathroom. I move as quickly and as far away from camp as possible. Only it's pointless. My stomach hurts too much, and I need to go now or I'll end up going all over myself. I am glad it's so dark out and no one can see me. I don't have time to dig a hole. Instead, I pull down my pants and go right where I stand, only a few feet away from camp. When I finish, I feel a little better but find myself returning to this exact spot two more times throughout the night.

I am not sure what time my fever breaks. Exhaustion gets the best of me, allowing me to finally sleep while hoping that whatever my body is going through improves by tomorrow.

CHAPTER 30

DAY 23 & 24 FKT ATTEMPT

July 26 - 9:18 a.m.

7.54 miles / 331 feet

5 hours, 8 minutes

"A mother's love for her child is like nothing else in the world. It knows no law, no pity, it dares all things and crushes down remorselessly all that stands in its path."
-Agatha Christie

ONCE THE SUN RISES, I find myself staring ahead of me at the mesh of my tent again. I feel even sicker today. I don't want to move, but I know I must. It's finally time to take my last Tylenol. The medicine paired with an anti-nausea pill will hopefully do the trick to jump-start my morning. I grab a packet of peanut butter and two crackers from my bear bag and begin to nibble away. I've read before that peanut butter can help calm an upset stomach. Hopefully, it will help treat my diarrhea. It is tough to eat, though, because I don't feel hungry. I take small sips of water to wash the peanut butter down and forgo the crackers. I know at most it is only 100 calories. *I need to eat*, I tell myself, but the thought of food makes my stomach turn. I try to eat more but can't, so I don't. Instead, I grab my water bottle and take my anti-nausea pill with the last of my Tylenol.

My energy drains completely, and I have to stop to regain my strength every few minutes to pack up. It is already nine before I finish getting ready to leave camp. The water and peanut butter I had eaten earlier have gone straight through me. I am forced to return to use the bathroom in the same place as last night. The hikers camped next to me are long gone, and no one is around to see. I dig a deep hole and bury my mess. It is beyond gross.

I take a look at my watch. I have only gone a mile in over an hour. I felt like I was flying yesterday morning in comparison to today. It's as though someone snapped my wings in half. I take another look at my phone. I begin to talk to myself. I should be able to reach a regular road today should I need help. I am still battling at the thought of actually calling for help. If I call to receive any aid from someone, setting the record is over. All my hard work and hard-fought battles that have gotten me to this point will have been for nothing. But is it all for nothing? I have learned so much about myself since the start of the trail. I stop and sit on a rock again. I still don't have it in me to quit. I don't want to. I love what I am doing too much. I message my mom on my inReach. I tell her I haven't been feeling well. She asks if I need her to meet me somewhere. I tell her no and that I will be okay. Deep down, I know it's a lie. A lie that I want to believe. I get off the rock and slowly begin to walk once again.

I begin to see runners and other weekend hikers after a few miles. Envy brews inside of me when I see runners moving quickly and freely without being weighed down by a pack. Seeing them gives me hope. It means I am near a trailhead. I turn my phone off airplane mode, thankful to have service. I call my mom. I wish her a Happy Birthday, but my mom knows me all too well. She can tell in my voice that something isn't right. I tell her I have been sick for the past two days. She tells me she can come and meet me if I need help. I am still optimistic, so tell her no again and that I will be okay. She tells me she is coming anyway. I finally agree. "Yes, Mom, please come." I then tell her I need to hang up because I have to go to the bathroom.

I find a tree not too far off the trail to shield me. My bowel movements have now turned to liquid. When I finish, I only make it a few more minutes before having to go again and again. I look at my watch. It has taken me four hours to go three miles, and the only energy I have left is draining quickly. I stop and rest every few minutes, trying to muster up the energy to continue. It is physically and mentally taxing. I call my mom back. I look at my Guthook app. There is parking at the Santiam Pass trailhead, near Highway 20, and not too far from here. I give my mom the coordinates. She tells me it will take her five hours to drive to me. I tell her that it's okay and thank her for making such a long drive. I am incredibly grateful for the amount of support she has given me. I find a nice boulder to sit on once again. Only this time, I remove my pack and take out a packet of pound cake. I manage to eat half of it. Still not enough calories. I wash it down with water and find just a little more strength to keep going.

It takes me over five hours to go the next seven miles. I am exhausted and dehydrated, but every time I take a sip of water,

I find myself having to go to the bathroom. The water seems to run straight through me. I begin feeling groggy. It is like I am in a daze and can't snap out of it. My vision seems off. Things don't look as crisp and clear as they had before. I promise myself that I can finally lie down and rest once I make it to the trailhead. Instead, I continue pushing forward in a zombie-like state, moving even slower than before.

When I finally arrive at the trailhead, I am happy to learn that there is a privy. A trail angel has placed several gallons of water at the nearby bench. I empty my water bottles and fill them up with clean water but still filtering them. I set up my sleeping mat near the privy. I take off my socks and shoes and elevate them on the tree next to me.

My mind and heart are still battling with giving up my FKT attempt. I have endured so much, and I know the smart thing to do is to call it off. My mom is already on her way. These past days have been sheer torture and have put me even further behind on mileage. I know I need help. I call my sister and ask her to book us a hotel room in Sisters, Oregon. I left my credit card with her to use for whatever our kids needed for the summer and strongly encourage her to use it to book our stay. She is the type of person who wouldn't use it or would tell me not to worry about it.

I then call my friend Rebecca and give her an update. She is all too kind and gives me several words of encouragement. She agrees that she won't update my status on the Women of the Mountain Facebook page until I have made up my mind about my next move.

Although I am sick, I am thankful for the privy right next to me. I use it several times. Each time I return to my sleeping mat and plop limply down. I am exhausted. I doze off for a few minutes and am woken up with the same aching in my stomach as the night before. I walk as quickly as possible to the privy with my feet only halfway slipped into my shoes. Only this time, I don't make it. I end up going in my underwear. I enter the privy to remove them in hopes nothing has made its way onto my pants. Luckily none has. This is the first time in my life I have ever had diarrhea this bad. I place my fecal matter-covered underwear in a Ziploc bag and put them on the outside of my pack. I grab my water bottle and scrub away at my hands and bottom. I then lather my hands up with hand sanitizer.

I try to think about what may have caused my distress. It can't be giardia. I had filtered my water every single time, except when I ate the snow near Mount Adams last week. I also use hand sanitizer like crazy. Maybe it's food poisoning from what I had eaten at Timberline Lodge. I felt sick the moment I left. I may have even been sick before I knew it, and the food there just intensified it. No matter my train of thought, my mind keeps circling back to giardia. The idea of a tiny parasite inside my stomach makes me feel even sicker. I know it can be caused by eating contaminated food or water and can even be found in soil. Perhaps I touched something contaminated. Maybe the water I have been drinking wasn't filtered enough. It is possible that a few drops of unfiltered water could have made their way to my mouth. It doesn't matter, though. What's done is done. I need to get healthy, so I can continue on, if I even can.

My mother shows up late in the evening. The look on her face when she sees me offers some validity that I made the right choice in having her pick me up. I am happy to learn that she has brought my kids with her. They are excited to see me and help load my gear into the car. With my socks still off, I don't bother to put my feet inside my shoes all the way, gently slipping the top part of my feet into them. When I reach the passenger's seat, I slide them off entirely. Although I stink, my mom doesn't say a word about the stench. Instead, she offers me some fries and a hamburger. With her strong motherly tone, she tells me to eat. I only nibble away at a few fries. I am still not hungry. I wish my mom another Happy Birthday and apologize for wasting her day with my rescue. She tells me kindly it's okay and I don't have to apologize.

When we arrive at the hotel, I keep my shoes off and walk barefoot inside. I lay on the floor of our room as my mom starts a bath for me. I don't have the energy to scrub away the filth caked on me, so I lie there soaking in the warm water. My daughter enters minutes later with Pedialyte, some antidiarrheals, Tylenol, probiotics, and vitamin C. She tells me that Grandma told her not to leave until I have taken the medicine and have finished the cup of Pedialyte. When I finish, my mom refills the cup, and my daughter enters the bathroom again. She has a smirk on her face and is enjoying being bossy all too much. I smile at her and finish what she has brought me. She returns a few more times, telling me Grandma told her to keep returning until I have finished the entire liter. She also scoops up my dirty clothes and gives them to my mom to wash.

It is already getting late before I exit the bathtub. I look in the mirror. I didn't think my stomach could be even more sunken in than before. Since my mother took all my clothes to wash, I have nothing to wear. I have lost so much weight I can fit into my ten-year-old son's boxer briefs. My mom also gives me her shirt to wear. My kids are fast asleep. I lay there tossing and turning and making several trips to the bathroom. I don't make it quick enough one of the times and again go in my underwear. I turn on the shower water and rush to clean up quickly. I wrap a towel around my waist and return to bed. Hours have passed before I finally fall asleep. I am unsure what time it is, but I know it is late when I feel a hand placed atop my forehead. It's my mom. She tells me I have a fever and gives me more medicine and Pedialyte to take. When I finish it, I fall back asleep. By morning, I am feeling better. My mother has always had a way of healing others. Her kindness and selflessness are what make her a great mother and nurse. I feel all too lucky to have her in my life.

CHAPTER 31

DAY 24

July 27 - 7:00 a.m.

0 miles / 0 feet

0 hours, 0 minutes

"Families are the compass that guides us.
They are the inspiration to reach great heights,
and our comfort when we occasionally falter."

-Brad Henry

TODAY IS MY DAUGHTER CAROLYNN'S NINTH BIRTHDAY. I give her a big hug and wish her a huge Happy Birthday. Although a part of me wants to get back on the PCT, I know I need to spend at least another day recovering. Of all the trials and tribulations that have happened to me on the trail, being able to spend this special day with her is what matters most. My mom nods in agreement as I share my decision to rest another day. We take our time getting ready in the morning and have the premade bags of food given to us from the hotel for breakfast since their dining facility is closed because of the Coronavirus.

For lunch, we drive to a nearby restaurant. My appetite is slowly returning. I still have diarrhea, but I'm going less frequently. My mom knows I feel better, so she finally shares her thoughts. "You know, Jess, when I first arrived to pick you up, you looked like a shriveled-up raisin and smelled unbearably bad," I laugh in agreement. "You look much better today, have more light in you, and a little more roundness in your cheeks." I smirk and take another nibble at my lunch.

After we finish lunch, we stop at the local grocery store. I stay in the car as my mom enters to buy my daughter a birthday cake and ice cream. We return to the hotel and my kids put on their swimsuits. We all hang out at the pool for a few hours. My mother and I sit, feet submerged in the hot tub, as we watch my kids enjoy swimming in the pool. I still feel weak, but I know my recovery is going well. With every sip of Pedialyte and water I take, I feel stronger. Being able to rest is also playing a significant role in getting back to my usual self.

We order pizza for dinner and sing "Happy Birthday" to both my daughter and mom. Then I watch my kids devour the cake and ice cream. I am able to eat a small slice of pizza and cake. When we head back to the hotel room, my mom tells us that she has brought all my daughter's presents to open, including the ones Tim and I had ordered for her a month prior. I am glad I get to enjoy the look on my daughter's face as she opens up her gifts. She begins to smirk as my mom hands her the first present. All eyes are on her as she slowly begins to remove the tape ever so carefully as not to tear the wrapping. Her brother and sister grow impatient yelling at her to just rip the paper off.

Her slow paper removal is eating away at them and she knows it. She knows what she is doing and is enjoying every minute of terrorizing her siblings. After the first present, she jokes that she was just kidding about the wrapping removal and tears the paper off of the rest of her presents within minutes. Once she is finished, my kids sit on the floor next to the beds playing with the new toys until it is time for them to sleep.

My mom and I stay up and have a thoughtful conversation. My mom tells me she prays for my safety on the trail and that her strength passes on to me when I feel weak. I try putting myself in her place and think about how worried I would be if one of my children were out on the trail hiking solo. I can only hope to share the same love and support towards whatever adventures my kids choose or don't choose when they are older.

I let her prayerful words sink into my soul, and I can't get over how incredibly blessed I have been since the start of the trail. She is such a selfless woman, and I hope that she ends up being blessed 100 times over compared to how much she has given me. I do my best to hold it together and take in all of her words of wisdom and kindness. It is a beautiful end to our evening.

CHAPTER 32

DAY 25 FEMALE FKT ATTEMPT

July 28 - 2:15 p.m.

17.4 miles / 2,484 feet

7 hours, 34 minutes

"The beautiful thing about setbacks is
they introduce us to our strengths."

-Robin Sharma

ALTHOUGH I AM NOT ONE HUNDRED PERCENT YET, the rest and re-fueling make me wake up feeling better than I have in several days. I have enough energy to go back on the trail. But since I still have recovery ahead of me, I won't be pushing myself on the PCT quite as hard as I previously had. I believe it will take me a while to get back to feeling like an athlete again.

Even though I missed the FKT attempt, I still have the Female Supported Fastest Known Time I can snag. And once my mind is made up, I make this new goal my purpose. First, I update my status on social media, making it official that my sickness forced me to drop out of my overall FKT attempt, but I won't be coming home yet. In doing so, I write the following:

"When it comes to the trail, whatever plans you had often go right out the door as soon as you take your first step. I learned this on day one when my siblings, cousin, and I were hit with a storm of rain and snow. From that day forward, I knew each mile would be hard-fought. You would think it unfair, or perhaps that I should have waited, but I would never take back any of the experiences I've had or the difficulties I've endured so far. I left Washington feeling strong, especially after ditching my winter gear. I had a couple of awesome forty-seven- and forty-four-mile days. However, after those two days, I woke up feeling terrible. I had a fever and felt incredibly sick. I have had rhabdomyolysis before, so I do not take pain relievers. So far, I have done this trail with hardly an ounce of pain relievers. And believe me, I've felt EVERYTHING! No worries, I don't have rhabdo now. But, after waking up feeling sick, I still had thirty miles to trek before I could receive any aid. As soon as I had phone signal, I called my mom. She lives in Washington and is an amazing nurse. I needed her advice and motherly love. She asked me if I needed her to come but told her I would be alright. That night, I had the worst fever and shakes I think I may have ever experienced. I slept in that morning and took my time packing up. What normally takes me fifteen minutes took me close to an hour. All my energy was depleted. I would hike for the next eleven hours and only make it twenty-two miles, struggling the entire way. I chugged two bottles of water, and for the first time during my hike, I finally took Tylenol. The next night went the same, and the following day, I called my mom because things seemed to be getting worse. (Just so happens, it was her birthday.) I asked her to come get me because I was incredibly ill. I hiked seven miles in almost five hours and stopped. I lay my mat out on the dirt and lay there awaiting her arrival. It would be a five-hour drive. As I lay there, I am feeling incredibly lucky and blessed. My family has been so supportive, and I can never repay what they have done for me and my kids. My amazing husband is deployed, so they have been watching our three kids so I can be out here. So, with the help of my mom and a few days in a hotel, I am starting to feel better. Things don't always go as planned, and I have been humbled beyond measure. I am extremely grateful for everyone's love, support, and amazing words of encouragement. I've had a few days to read your comments, and I cannot thank you all enough. This does not mean my adventure has come to an end. But because I had to receive medical attention, it changes my FKT status to Supported status. So, now those of you who wanted to come say hi or bring me a snack are more than welcome!"

The amount of love and supportive responses I receive in return is remarkable. I have a friend who lives near Crater Lake. Once she sees my post, she offers to meet me on the trail and help with whatever I may need. Since my FKT status has now changed, and I can have people join to help me, I respond in excitement. We make plans to meet at Crater Lake in a few days.

Before leaving for the trail, my family and I make a quick stop at the local market. I grab a few snacks, some hot mint cocoa, and make peanut butter and jelly sandwiches for lunch, stuffing a few extra into my pack's side mesh. I will only need to carry a three-day supply of food before reaching my next resupply. My mom also stocks me with vitamins and Tylenol should I need any more along the way. By two, I am finally back on the PCT. We drive to the exact spot where I had left. By FKT rules, I must start back at the same point as where I left. My kids and mother join me for a small section of it until we reach Highway 20, where I must cross. We laugh and enjoy each other's company until it is time to say our farewells.

I spend the rest of the afternoon listening to voicemails. My family and friends' support and words of encouragement make it all worthwhile being out here. Rebecca left a voicemail asking me how I was doing and had nothing but kind words to say. She also says her niece wants to know if I think it is better to hike alone or with someone. I am thankful for this question and spend a few hours contemplating my response. In the end, I respond with the following:

"I think there is a certain type of strength gained when you hike by yourself versus with someone else. When you're with someone else, you can lean on them in moments of weakness and draw strength and motivation from one another. There is also someone to joke around with and someone to look after you. When you are by yourself, you don't have anyone to lean on. You have to find that strength within. It is surprising how much stronger and more capable we are than we think. You also have to motivate yourself and when you are down, find the will and strength to push on. I don't think there is a right answer as to which is better. It all depends on what your goals are and what you are trying to accomplish." As I finish my thoughts, the trail starts to become rockier and the trees soon become minimal.

In all of Oregon, this trail section is my favorite. The PCT turns into a field of lava rock overlooking the Three Sisters Mountain Range. The heat radiating from the rocks is intense, making me grateful I am hiking this section now. I can't imagine how hot it gets during the afternoon. The sun is beginning to set, and I am soon met with a lone tree in this field of heated lava rock. The different shades of reds bouncing off the rocks make the greenness of the tree's beauty stand out even more. For some reason, I feel a connectedness with this tiny yet mighty tree. Although it looks to be all alone, I know it is not. Something has protected it and helped it grow. Maybe faith, prayer, luck, who knows? I wonder what trials and tribulations it has battled to make it this far? It is a true symbol of my hike. The tree rises tall as though saying, "Look at me. I am still standing. No matter how harsh the terrain or weather, I am still here." The tree's ability to make it this far only signifies the strength of this tiny yet mighty tree. I take a brief moment and thank the tree for being there, and offer a small prayer.

Just then, flashes of lightning catch my eye. There is a thunderstorm over the Three Sisters Mountain Range. The storm doesn't make its way towards this open field of lava rock.

Today has been a long water carry. I haven't been able to refill my bottles since I left my family. When I look at my Guthook application, I only have a few miles left before reaching a tree-covered camp area. Previous entries state the possibility of trail magic. When I reach the shaded campsite at mile 669, several hikers have already set up for the night. Sadly, whatever trail magic lay here before is long gone. I will have to wait until morning to make it to the next available water source. Most campsites are also taken up, and I find myself walking in a circle until I find a big enough area to set up. Unfortunately, it is next to another backpacker who is already fast asleep. When I am set up for the night, I am filled with joy. I am happy I was able to continue my trek even though I know tomorrow I will be hiking exactly where I had seen the lightning tonight. Hopefully, the weather holds up.

CHAPTER 33

DAY 26 FEMALE FKT ATTEMPT

July 29 - 6:52 a.m.

33.9 miles / 5,010 feet

15 hours, 4 minutes

"Health is not valued 'til sickness comes."

-Thomas Fuller

I STILL HAVE HALF A WATER BOTTLE LEFT, but by morning I am parched. I drink most of it. I have two miles to go before reaching my next water point, which turns out to be a mucky pond. I've traveled over twenty miles only carrying the water from the time I left my family. Once I reach the pond, I filter an entire bottle of water and quickly down it all. I top off another bottle and filter just this one to carry. I know South Mathieu Lake has to be a cleaner water source, and it's only another mile and a half further from where I am now.

Sources prove me correct when I reach the lake. I refill one bottle and once again drink it all. I then grab handfuls of water to wash the dirt off my legs, feet, face, and arms. I take a moment to

199

sit and enjoy the stillness of the lake. I finish the rest of my breakfast and make two bottles of PERC Coffee with some chocolate Silverstar Nutrition Protein to go. My appetite has not yet returned completely, and I'm still having trouble eating an entire meal. The hike between today's water sources isn't too far, allowing me to carry less weight.

Still affected by giardia, I use the restroom more often than I would like. By noon, blood appears in my stool, and I get scared. I message my husband on my inReach to get his advice about the blood. Being a Physician Assistant, he eases my mind by telling me most likely the blood was caused by going to the restroom so many times. However, for peace of mind, he recommends I see a doctor. I plan to hike to a well-known campground tonight. From there, I can hitch a ride into town tomorrow morning to get treated.

All circumstances aside, I find myself enjoying the time I am spending in the Three Sisters Mountain Range. Black obsidian rocks fill the fields, which is something I have never seen in person. I reach down and pick up a large piece. I drag my finger gently across its sharp yet smooth edge. The rock looks and feels like glass. I can see why the people before us used this rock as a source for weaponry such as arrowheads. I then place the rock back down in the same spot I found it.

Hiking a little further, I spot a U.S. Forest Service sign stating that this section is an Obsidian Limited Entry Area. A permit is required to enter, but my Pacific Crest Trail permit allows me entry. The amount of obsidian in this area is far greater than where I had picked up the piece to look at previously. It is scattered all along and across the trail. Before today and even in all my research, I never knew this place existed.

Further ahead is the Obsidian Falls, which pours directly over a field of shattered obsidian. The falls are not too far off from the trail but require a steep descent to reach them. I don't bother hiking down and admire it from a distance.

By the end of the day, I've tallied fifteen bottles I've taken in today. I know being sick has dehydrated me, so I make it a point to drink as much water as possible. I mixed half of the bottles with peach tea flavor packets. By evening I started peeing frequently, and my appetite feels normal. My energy hasn't completely returned just yet, and I know a big part of it is from my lack of calories, so I make a point to pack in calories when I can. I have spaghetti for dinner and wash it down with my Silver Star Nutrition vanilla protein powder, which makes a huge difference in how much energy I now have. I begin to want even more food as my energy levels start to increase.

As the sun sets, I make the 1.3-mile hike down to the Elk Lake Resort. I search for the camp host, but I can't find him anywhere. I go ahead and find the PCT camp area. The campsite is not very big but has a few reserved spots. I set my tent up next to another hiker and fall asleep with ease, hoping that tomorrow the doctor tells me the blood in my stool is the cause of an irritated bowel.

CHAPTER 34

July 30 - 3:56 p.m.

19.2 miles / 2,372 feet

6 hours, 9 minutes

"One genuine connection can make
you feel at home in an unfamiliar place."

-Anonymous

IT HAS BEEN A LONG, PEACEFUL NIGHT, and when morning finally arrives, I walk to the resort's restaurant to grab breakfast I don't have to make myself. However, when I get there, I am sad to learn that it won't open until noon. So, I munch on a breakfast bar instead and walk over to a bench near the lake.

I try to call an Uber to pick me up, but I can't find one, at least none showing up on my application. I am not comfortable with asking a stranger from this resort for a ride into town. I search the PCT Central Oregon Trail Angel Facebook page in hopes there are trail angels available to offer rides. A member from the group privately messages me and tells me that she is free for the day and can give me a ride wherever I need to go. She responds with, "Hi! If you don't want to hitch, I can pick you up. And you're welcome to hang out at our house today (shower/laundry/etc.) Also, happy to drive you around town for resupply errands. Let me know!"

As though a weight lifts off of me, I am all too relieved at this trail angel's kindness. When she arrives, we take a few minutes to greet one another as her golden retriever swims in and out of the water fetching the stick she is throwing. The trail angel looks to be around the same age as me. She seems fit and is a bit taller than me. She smiles as we talk, and after a few minutes, we leave the resort. We first reach her home, where I shower, plug in all of my electronics, and wash my clothes. While waiting for my laundry to finish washing, she offers me fresh fruit and a ride into town. We switch my clothes over to the dryer, and I tell her about my situation with giardia. She tells me that she doesn't mind taking me to a nearby urgent care.

When the doctor finally examines me, I tell him about my bout with giardia and how my stool is yellowish and has blood. I learn that I only weigh 117.2 pounds, fully clothed. This means I have lost almost twenty pounds since the start of the trail. My blood pressure is 98/64. Normal blood pressure is around 120/80, but I am not too worried about it because mine is usually on the low end. Although there is blood in my stool, the doctors are unable to do anything for me. They tell me that it is the cause of irritation, and since I am still on the trail, they don't want to prescribe me any antibiotics. If I had an adverse reaction to them, getting help would be difficult because I would be in the middle of nowhere. They tell me that, over time, the blood should dissipate. If it doesn't improve, then I will need to seek further medical attention. My husband had told me this exact thing, and I feel like I just wasted half of my day for nothing. However, being seen in person gives me greater ease of mind. I thank the doctors for their help and leave for lunch.

Next, the trail angel takes me to a fantastic local spot for lunch. It's in a food-truck park, so I have lots of options. I decide on a hamburger, fries, and a bottle of water. I also order a large pepperoni deep dish pizza to go. We then head to a sporting goods store, where I buy a new water filter and throw away my old one, keeping one for backup. Then she takes me by a grocery store for more food. I buy a couple of water bottles so I can toss out my old ones, some fresh peaches, and Ziploc bags for my pizza. I still have plenty of food to get me through to my next resupply point, so I don't buy much, but having fresh food for a change is worth the money spent. Before leaving the store, I check out some money to repay the trail angel for her kindness and order a Frappuccino. I realize that my appetite is back, and I'm determined to throw down some calories. We then head back to the trail angel's house.

We both munch on berries while I finish packing up all my things. It feels terrific to change into my fresh and clean-smelling clothes. We hop in her vehicle to head back out to the trail. I offer her the money I had checked out, but she is so gracious and tells me not to worry about it. I give her a big smile and thank her for all that she has done. We make it to the trail-head by four. Before setting off, she gives me a bag of fresh blueberries. She tells me about the amazing pizza at Shelter Cove roughly fifty miles away. She says that if I get any to let her know if I think it is better than the pizza I bought earlier.

It is a 1.3-mile hike back up from where I left off yesterday. Once I start sweating, though, my body starts itching. I try to ignore it and push on. Unfortunately, my pack has also begun to rub against my back. I tuck my shirt into my pants to help stop the chafing, but it only helps a little. I am amazed at the blazing orange sunset. I wish I were high up on a mountain taking it all in, but for now, I will have to enjoy it through the trees of this densely wooded area.

When night arrives, I find that I don't care too much for this section. There are a lot of trees blocking my view of the night sky. With my headlamp on, I also get several glimpses of eyes shining back at me along the way. One set of eyes begins to follow alongside me, creeping me out even more. Its eyes are low to the ground, and the way it is moving makes me think it is a mountain lion. I let out a loud, "Hey!" and it runs off. By ten, I am ready to make camp and set up my tent for the evening. I find a nice tree well away from camp to hang my bear bag. There are several mosquitos out, so I move as quickly as possible.

Once inside my tent, I change into my sleeping clothes. As I lay there trying to fall asleep, I hear footsteps outside my tent in the trail's direction. Thinking it is another hiker, I yell, "Hello!?" Only, no one responds. Whatever was there has either stopped in their tracks or has runoff. I yell out another, "HEY!" hoping to scare off whatever was or is still out there.

I struggle to fall asleep as I find myself itching relentlessly. I eventually remove my leggings and top, and the itching goes away. It is then that I realize that whatever detergent the trail angel used on my clothes has not agreed with my skin. I have never been allergic to detergent before and wonder what kind it is. When I finally fall asleep, it is not long before I am awoken by what sounds like two animals huffing. *Maybe black bears*, I think to myself. However, after a few minutes, the noises disappear. I try not to overthink it and can't wait for the morning to arrive so I can leave this area.

CHAPTER 35

DAY 28 FEMALE FKT ATTEMPT

July 31 - 5:58 a.m.

37.9 miles / 5,092 feet

15 hours, 18 minutes

"If you think you are too small to make
a difference, try sleeping with a mosquito."

-Dalai Lama

I WAKE UP A LITTLE AFTER FIVE with a strong urge to use the restroom. My bowel movement still has blood in it but far less than the day prior. My stool is also returning to a normal color. It is not as yellow as it had been previously. There are a lot of mosquitos out, making it difficult to go to the bathroom. I put my head net on and swat them away from my bottom as much as possible.

I am still sleepy. With all the commotion happening around me last night, I did not sleep well. But the sunrise makes me forget about how tired I am. This morning's light is as stunning as last night's sunset, bright and blazing orange, reminding me of fire. I have pizza for breakfast and will eat the remaining slices throughout the day, which also helps me accomplish one of my bucket list items, "Eat a large pizza in one day."

Once again, my pack starts rubbing and chafing the right side of my lower back. I stop and take a look and rub Trail Toes cream over it. After a few more minutes of hiking, it continues rubbing. Although the Trail Toes has done a fantastic job of preventing further blistering on my feet, it can only do so much for my back. I stop and remove my pack to take a look. My back is red, and the skin has started breaking. I pull out my first aid kit, grab a bandage, and place it over the area. Usually, my pants protect this area on my lower back, but I have lost so much weight they have begun to fall off, despite holding my size zero pants up with a carabiner. I try tightening them even more, but it's pointless. They fall back down, resting just below my hips.

As I continue, my pack begins rubbing against the left side of my back now. Again, I stop to take a look. It looks the same as my other side, both red and raw. I place a Band-Aid over it. I then try to reconfigure my pack to prevent it from rubbing. I move the blue foam sit pad that usually rests against my back further down for added padding to the blistered area and tighten the hip belt. With all of the weight I've shed, I can't cinch down my shoulder straps any further, which would easily fix the problem. But after hiking a few more minutes, I realize it is all pointless. I haven't found a way to stop my pack from rubbing me raw. I spend all morning trying to make the proper adjustments, but nothing helps. With over thirty days of hiking under my belt, this pack issue is now a real concern.

It's still early in the morning, and I cross paths with a crew camped out on a dirt road that intersects the PCT. I learn there is a female attempting to set the Oregon PCT Fastest Known Time record. A woman from her crew offers me water and helps refill my water bottles. I talk with a few of the crew members, who also offer me some donuts and a warm cup of coffee. The donuts are a nice surprise because they also happen to be my favorite. I thank them for their generosity and leave with a cup of warm coffee, maple bar, and chocolate sprinkled donut.

By late afternoon, I reach Shelter Cove. The resort has an area set up just for PCT hikers. There is a charging station and hiker box. The box is full of things other hikers are tired of and don't want to carry anymore. It is a great way to get rid of unwanted items while at the same time find wanted items. Ramen noodles and tuna packets fill the bins. I charge my phone and grab a few tuna packets. No matter how many I've had, I don't grow tired of them. Lemon Pepper Albacore is my favorite flavor.

I then visit the Shelter Cove Restaurant and order the largest chili cheese hotdog on the menu and a soda. It was a 1.8-mile hike down to get to here, which in turn adds 1.8 miles straight back up the trail. Although I am not thrilled about the added 3.6 miles, I am happy about the delicious food I have just ordered. I am sick of pizza. I still have two pizza slices left to complete my bucket list item. I hadn't planned to order any as the trail angel suggested, but the hikers next to me have generously offered me the two slices they have left. I gladly take the slices and place them into Ziploc bags for later. When I finish eating, I head into the store and pick up a few more food items.

Shelter Cove has Wi-Fi, allowing me to message my family. I give them all updates and post a few photos to social media. After resting for two hours, it is time to go even though I would much rather spend the evening here. I dream of all the things I could do: shower, laundry, message friends. But there is still a lot of light left in my day, and I know I should push ahead. It is slow hiking back up from where I left off. The chafing on my back has worsened no matter how many times I stop to fix my bandages and rearrange my pack.

When I am back on the trail, I begin a 2,000-foot climb up towards Mount Yoran. My goal is to get the majority of the climb finished today to make tomorrow's hike easier. Unfortunately, the trail is littered with mosquitos, forcing me to put on my head net. The pests begin biting me through my shirt. I am beyond annoyed, so I put on my raincoat because I know they can't bite through it. My raincoat, paired with having to climb, makes me hot and sweaty. It's a pain, but I would much rather sweat than be devoured by mosquitos.

When I reach the Mount Yoran Trail Junction, mile marker 752.9, I set up my tent for the night. But I can't get over the incredible number of mosquitos in this area. I get inside my tent as quickly as possible, and once I am inside, I can hear them buzzing around, trying to figure out how to get in. I scan the entire tent, squishing three.

My extreme dislike for mosquitos started when I was a child. I was sleeping next to my aunt when she woke up to a mosquito bite on her eyelid. She couldn't even open her eye. The amount of swelling and itching it caused her is enough to terrify any five-year-old kid. From then on, I have always been paranoid of waking up to the same nightmarish ordeal.

I still have two slices of pizza left before reaching my goal. I should have eaten them before brushing my teeth. I do my best to finish them off so that I can tick off another bucket list item. When I finish eating, I do a mental celebratory dance. I crawl out of my tent and hang my bear bag far from camp. I circle around, keeping as many mosquitos off as possible while still brushing my teeth. I hobble back over, enter, and once again search for mosquitos. This time, only one has managed to make its way inside.

I try wearing my sleep clothes, but again I find myself itching uncontrollably. The only thing I can do is take them off and sleep in my underwear. I also take off the bandages from my back to air out my open wounds. Both are about the size of a notecard. My left side is deeper than my right. I grimace every time my sleeping quilt brushes against them. I struggle to keep anything from touching them.

Normally before going to bed every night, I make a goal of making it to a specific campsite I had planned that morning. Unfortunately, I've learned through this experience that I most often fail at any of my planned destinations. Weather, terrain, and physical exhaustion have curtailed my goals of the long distances I was expecting to cover on this hike. So, instead, I now focus on the elevation and marker points for the next thirty to forty miles.

CHAPTER 36

August 1 - 7:32 a.m.

38.5 miles / 5,659 feet

14 hours, 18 minutes

"At some point, you just pull off the Band-Aid,
and it hurts, but then it's over and you're relieved."
-John Green

WHEN MORNING ARRIVES, my wounds have scabbed over, but they have stuck to my quilt. With my teeth clenched, I slowly and gently attempt to pull it away. Not having any luck with the slow removal, I rip the material away from my back in one shaky motion. I feel on fire and fall to my stomach, breathing heavily, waiting for the pain to subside. It feels exactly like road rash, reminding me of when I crashed my bike during a race. While my family and I were stationed in Baumholder, Germany, Tim and I participated in a sprint triathlon in Heidelberg. When we reached the bike portion of the race, it involved a long climb up to the Heidelberg castle. Once I made my way to the top, I took the downhill fearlessly. Unfortunately, I tried to defy the laws of physics and failed terribly. I attempted to pass a competitor on a turn. My momentum carried me further to the outside of the road. My tires carried so close to the edge, I eventually ran into the curb, which caused my bike to tip. Once down, I slowly stood up, wiggling my legs and arms to make sure nothing broke. I got back on my bike with messed-up shifters and coasted to the transition area. Adrenaline pumping, I had yet to notice how much road rash covered my body. People stared as I was running. My knees and elbows were full of blood. It wasn't until I finished my run that my husband said my cheeks, covered in blood, were also hanging out of my triathlon shorts. I was in pure agony once I came off of my adrenaline. The following week was sheer torture.

Right now, my back feels on fire, the exact same way it did during that race. It throbs and is tender to touch, but I know I need to take care of it just as I had to with my road rash. Preventing infection is key to healing. I open the small tube of bacitracin from my first aid kit and rub it over the open wounds. I then grab four Band-Aids connecting them into pairs. I place them over my wounds and tape around the outside of them so they cannot come off. Once I pack up, I am slow to put my hiking pack on. I know that it will rub against my back, and I know it is going to hurt. I build up the mental courage to finally put it on. The bandages seem to help a little. Unlike the previous days, they don't come off. I have made sure of it. It is painful, but I eventually become numb to it.

The morning chill braces me for the start of my day, but the 300-foot climb quickly warms me up. For breakfast, I eat the two slices of pizza given to me from the day before, along with some PERC Coffee mixed with mint cocoa. The trail angel was right. This pizza is a lot tastier than the one I had ordered when I was with her. I snap a photo of me devouring it to send to her later. Even more so, I just discovered a new love. Mint has always been a favorite of mine. Whether it's chocolate, ice cream, or hard candy, I have always loved it. Pairing the mint cocoa with PERC Coffee for breakfast was something out of this world. A part of me wanted to make up another batch, but I held back. It will be something to look forward to for tomorrow.

As the morning progresses, the mosquitos vanish, and beautiful views greet me. I take a deep breath. As I exhale, I take a look around until I finally focus on what lies ahead. There is a little bit of snow atop the nearby peaks. From here, I can see for miles. Mountains lay upon mountains, and trees lay upon trees. It feels endless. The vastness of the woods and remoteness of this location makes me feel so small, yet, I have never felt so connected with the land and my emotions. I reach down to touch the Earth, grabbing a handful of dirt.

My Uncle Ira and Aunt Minnie have taught me to give thanks to our creator and Mother Earth, pronounced "Chalkum" in Blackfeet. It wasn't until I started hiking before I truly understood the meaning. Usually, I should take a pinch of tobacco and a small piece of Earth. I don't have tobacco, so I just use the dirt. I hold it up to my heart and raise it into the air and back towards my heart. I begin to pray and give thanks. I started doing this a few days before reaching Oregon. I don't even know if what I am doing is correct, but it feels right in my heart. When I finish, I take what I have been holding, carve out a small hole in the ground, and bury the dirt, giving it back to Mother Earth for her care. My aunt and uncle had told me to do this along my route in places I feel are special or challenging. This place is definitely extraordinary.

I have a long water carry once I leave Summit Lake, almost ten miles from where I started this morning. From here, it is roughly eighteen miles to the next reliable water source. Afraid of running out of water, I grab my empty two-liter collapsible bottle, and for the first time on the trail, I fill it up. I don't leave the lake until I fill all my water bottles and drink an entire bottle myself. My shoulders cry at the amount of weight I have just added to my pack. Finally, after thirteen miles since leaving Summit Lake, where I last filled up, I make it to a trailhead easily accessible by car. To my surprise, there are over two dozen five-gallon water jugs.

A trail angel has also placed several plastic bins full of items hikers may need, including tape, Band-Aids, toilet paper, pads, battery packs, and more. The trail angels have left a note asking for hikers not to take the battery packs, only recharge as you need and return the battery packs when done. *Wow, this is amazing,* I think to myself. I grab three packets of mosquito repellent wipes and a couple of giant Band-Aids, placing them into the side mesh of my pack. I also refill three water bottles.

As the day progresses, I cross paths with more hikers heading northbound and am all too happy to tell them about the amazing trail magic ahead. By evening, I pick a tent site that should have cell phone service. Reports on the Guthook guide also state that the sunrise is stunning from there. As I reach the site, I notice three other tents already set up for the night. It is a giant campsite, but there is only one spot left. Since my site is so close to the mountain's edge, it's very windy, so I have a little trouble grounding the tent.

Once inside my tent, I take my time peeling off my bandages from my back. They are glued to my skin, especially on the right side. I let out several deep breaths and a few low moans while gingerly removing them from my skin. When they are finally off, I place more bacitracin on my back and lay on my stomach.

I message my husband, my mom, Rebecca, and Hillary. I tell Hillary I will be in Crater Lake tomorrow evening. She asks me what food I would like to eat, and it doesn't take me long to decide. I ask her for chicken with mashed potatoes and a soda. Thinking of this meal makes my stomach growl. I then message the trail angel. I tell her that I did try the pizza from Shelter Cove, and it was far tastier than I had imagined. I also sent her a photo. When I am finished messaging everyone, I turn my phone off. I then turn slowly onto my side to sleep. I make it a point to do a better job of not letting my quilt touch my back. After a long hike tomorrow, I'm hoping I'll be feasting on some greasy, delicious chicken.

CHAPTER 37

August 2 - 5:59 a.m.

43 miles / 3,766 feet

14 hours, 38 minutes

"Every act of creation is first an act of destruction."

-Pablo Picasso

WHEN MORNING ARRIVES, I am not disappointed. The view from here is phenomenal. Shades of pinks and blues are beginning to light up the sky with the rise of the sun. I don't stay to watch it completely rise. I am on a mission today. I plan to make it to Crater Lake, where I will meet with Hillary. So, I pack up my things and begin my day.

I reach a wooden sign at mile 792.3. The sign is decorated with different colored flags and reads: "OR/WA HIGH PT. 7560'." I snap a few photos to remember the moment before I am back on my way. Finally, I feel like myself today. My stool is back to normal, and my energy and appetite have completely returned. I even pick up my pace, excited to see my friend.

I cross a road and enter Crater Lake, where I spot a Pacific Crest National Scenic Trail register. I write my name: "Flys High." In the comments section, I write, "SOBO Baby!" The hiker above has commented, "Goonies Never Die," and I write back, "Love that movie!" I then message my friend, Hillary, telling her that I won't make it to where we had planned previously until really late in the evening. I ask her if she can pick me up in a few hours, just twenty miles from where I had started this morning. She agrees to meet me at Highway 209, where the trail crosses.

At our meet-up location, I sit and wait on a nearby log. I remove one water bottle from my pack and wash my face. I then remove my shoes and begin to wash away the filth on my feet. I change into my sleep shirt so I don't smell as bad. After fifteen minutes, Hillary arrives, delicious meal in hand. Her three younger boys are also with her. I can't thank her enough for the fantastic meal and apologize if I stink. She tells me not to worry and that I smell okay. I begin to devour the food as though I have never eaten before. With my appetite back, I have eaten almost everything in my pack. Soda with ice tastes all too amazing. I stuff my face with biscuits, mashed potatoes, and chicken, then wash it down with my soda and repeat. Hillary chuckles as she drives me to the Mazama Village for resupply, where I buy enough snacks to hold me over the next couple of days.

On the drive back, we make a quick stop to see Crater Lake, the deepest lake in America. Unfortunately, the Pacific Crest Trail does not coincide with the lake. Instead, it goes completely around, missing it. It is something I wish could change because it is a beautiful site to see. Without Hillary, I'd have missed it altogether. The lake feels intense. I had visited here just a year ago in this exact spot with my children, admiring its baby blue color. When we finish taking photos, Hillary returns me to where I left the trailhead earlier. We plan to meet up again in a few days.

By 5:15 p.m., I am hiking the PCT again. It isn't long before the trail becomes a burn area. According to my guide, this burn field goes on for several miles. All campsites in the area have been closed for safety reasons. No one wants a dead tree falling on them in the middle of the night while they sleep. I plan to hike until I find a safe enough place to sleep. The hours tick by in a flash, and by eleven, I still have not made it to a campsite I am comfortable with or even one that is open.

When I reach the trailhead near the Crater Lake Highway, there are two vans surrounded by people who look to be the same age as me. I ask if I can hitch a ride into Mazama Village. I will camp there tonight. But the strangers tell me they don't have the room and are done for the evening. I turn back to the road and hike the rest of the way into the village. My feet hurt and walking on pavement doesn't help the situation. They ache, and I can feel another blister forming. It takes me a while to find the PCT campsite. By midnight, I am finally set up. I am spent and ready to fall asleep, too tired to remove the bandages from my back and feet. I end up leaving them on.

As I lay on my sleep mat, I revisit my day. It was amazing getting the opportunity to spend some time with my friend and see Crater Lake together. I haven't seen Hillary since we were stationed in El Paso, Texas. I have also been longing for fatty calories and am glad the greasy food Hillary brought me didn't upset my stomach.

CHAPTER 38

August 3 - 7:41 a.m.

34.4 miles / 4,698 feet

13 hours, 35 minutes

"Never regret. If it's good, it's wonderful.
If it's bad, it's experience."

-Victoria Holt

I SLEEP IN and take my time getting ready. I really want breakfast, but the nearby Mazama Village Store doesn't open until eight. It will be worth the wait, though, because the restrooms at the campsite are immaculate. They are actual restrooms and have running water and electrical outlets. The sink is a perfect place to wash up. I plug my power banks in next to a sink and take my time getting clean. I scrub away the filth on my hands, legs, and face. A blister has formed on my left pinky toe and the back of my heel. I pop both of them and wash my feet off with warm water. I then remove the bandages on my back and clean my wounds. I smother them with bacitracin and place a clean bandage over them. I only have a couple of Band-Aids left. I use a few paper towels to dry off. I also learn that the hiker boxes are near the PCT camp area. I rummage through them and score a few amazing items, my favorite being mint chocolate chip gum! I refill all my water bottles at a nearby spigot. Today will be my longest water carry at twenty miles.

When the store finally opens, I am one of the first to enter. I find the first aid section, but the Band-Aids aren't big enough for the wounds on my back. Then I see some panty liners on the bottom shelf. *Perfect!* I say to myself. They should be big enough for my wounds. I buy the panty liners, a cup of hot coffee, and an entire bag of bagels. They don't carry any Dr. Pepper, so I settle for a root beer. I eat two bagels while walking back to the trailhead from last night. My foot aches so badly today, and I attempt to walk on the dirt alongside the road to ease the pain. I also adjust my gait by shifting my weight to the right side of my foot, but this only seems to cause more anguish. I try to walk as normally as possible, hoping that the pain will eventually go away. After walking a quarter of a mile, a mail van slows down beside me. It is a couple who runs the post office at the Mazama Village, and they give me a ride to the trailhead.

When I have made it out of Crater Lake National Park, the woods begin to vanish. They have turned into another burn area. I spread out my water intake by drinking one full bottle every five miles. With every step I take, I am met with grasshoppers jumping in front and alongside me. The crackling noises made by their wings are a welcoming sound. There is no shade in the area, and it is a nice distraction from the heat.

Once I am back in the tree line, hiking up towards Devil's Peak, I cross paths with weekend backpackers. They are carrying an absurd amount of gear, making my back hurt just by looking at them. One guy has an actual stereo in hand, while another lady has a beach chair attached to her hiking pack. My best guess is they had not planned on hiking this far, or perhaps they just enjoy the glamping life too much.

This heavily packed couple reminds me of my first backpacking trip three years ago. We were a group of five, backpacking to the Enchantments in Leavenworth, Washington. To this day, it is still my favorite place on Earth. Completely inexperienced, we all packed what we thought we needed. My pack weighed almost fifty pounds alone. I brought a change of clothes for every day, a hammock, a chair, a mirror, a giant toiletry bag, and a lot more items I am sure ultralight backpackers would have a field day joking about. The climbing and weight of our packs was a challenge, causing us to stop and take breaks more times than we wanted. Lucky for us, we only had to make it to the one campsite. We would spend the next three days exploring the surrounding area, only returning to our tents at night to sleep. I would return the following year more educated and experienced, making it to the exact same spot in less than half the time.

As I begin to pass the overpacked hikers on a climb, they stop and ask for help. They are lost, and out of all the things they are carrying, they haven't packed a map. I pull out my phone and give them directions to the location they are trying to reach. They are almost a mile away from their planned destination and have made this climb for nothing. They thank me and begin to hike back down the mountain.

My hike up to Devil's Peak feels easy in comparison to the mountain ranges in Washington. The switchbacks seem gradual. I am able to climb with ease while enjoying all that surrounds me. There are white fluffy Pasque flowers alongside the trail, reminding me of my kids. When they were toddlers, I would read Dr. Seuss books to them almost every night. These flowers look exactly like the truffula trees in the children's book, *The Lorax*.

Giant western salsify covers the area and have turned into wish flowers bigger than my hand. I pick a salsify, and with one big breath, blow as many seeds off as I can. It takes me three full breaths before every single seed is gone and I can make a wish. I watch the seeds being carried away by the wind. If my kids were here, they would be having a blast at seeing who can get all the seeds off with the least amount of breaths. I grab one more flower, trying to beat my previous record. I smile as though I accomplished some giant feat, because this time, it only takes me two blows.

I don't cross paths with anyone until nightfall. Then, my mind wanders back to the lost backpackers, wondering what they would have done had I not shown up. It is incredibly easy to miss a turn, and without cell phone service or a satellite communicator, you can get lost. Hopefully, they made it safely to their destination.

By evening, I have found a nice campsite near the Sky Lakes Trail Junction. I wake in the middle of the night to the noise of something lurking around my tent. About a month ago, according to my Guthook guide, a cougar had circled another hiker's tent for two hours. They had camped just two miles before where I set up camp. The thought of a cougar being a few feet away makes my heart beat faster. I take a few deep breaths, slowly exhaling, trying to calm my nerves. I take another deep breath, this time letting out a loud, "Hey!" as I exhale. I do this a few more times until the footsteps eventually go away. With the thought of a cougar nearby, I have trouble falling asleep again. I lie silently in bed with my senses heightened, trying to listen for any noise.

CHAPTER 39

DAY 32 FEMALE FKT ATTEMPT

August 4 - 6:24 a.m.

30.7 miles / 2,723 feet

10 hours, 1 minute

"There is nothing more beautiful than someone who goes out of their way to make life beautiful for others."

-Mandy Hale

MY ABRASIONS LOOK BETTER TODAY, hurting just a little bit less. I place new bandages over them before heading off. Today is a low mileage day. In exactly thirty-one miles, Hillary will pick me up. Unfortunately, I greet the morning with thousands of mosquitos buzzing around. I rub the mosquito repellent wipes over my arms and clothes to keep them from biting at me. My pack also begins to dig into my left side, causing me to stop twice to readjust it.

I hike just outside of Fish Lake, mile 880. I thank whoever made the dirt path ahead of me. There are thousands of jagged lava rocks lining both sides of the trail. The dirt fills in the cracks between them, preventing the onset of scrambling. The heat radiating off the rocks is intense, feeling like the sun is blasting me from all directions. I am excited for the reprieve once I make it back to the tree line and into a shaded area. Today has been hot and is only supposed to get hotter from here. I don't know if I am ready for California heat just yet.

I hike the thirty-one miles in precisely ten hours and one minute, making it to our meet-up location a lot sooner than I had anticipated. The trail has been flat and fast today, allowing for another personal time and distance record. I find a nice log near the paved road and begin to stretch out my tired, achy legs. A female hiker heading in the opposite direction soon passes by with a confused look on her face. Before crossing the road, she asks if I am trying to hitch a ride from here because vehicles barely drive by. I smile and say, "No. I have a friend picking me up."

"Oh good," she says and carries on. I watch her walk down the trail, taking notice of her appearance. I can tell she is a thru-hiker. The more I hike, the easier it is to tell the difference. Most thru-hikers have a smell to them in comparison to weekend backpackers. Our clothes are also dusty or caked in grime from all the mileage we have put on them. Hiking packs have fewer things hanging off of them, and shoes are sometimes worn and weathered.

Hillary arrives at 4:30 p.m., welcoming me with a giant cup of icy cold Dr. Pepper. She has a two liter next to her in case I need a refill. The sugar and cold are a welcomed taste and energy booster. I slowly sip away at the delicious beverage, enjoying every gulp. We make a few stops along the way before reaching her home, starting at McDonald's, where I order a McChicken, large French fry, and an Oreo blizzard. I never thought I would enjoy eating McDonald's so much. Next, we head to a grocery store. Hillary joins me as I begin to pick out enough food to last me three days. Shopping is a lot different when thru-hiking and is a complete one-eighty from foods I might usually buy. I find myself focusing on items that are high in calories and fat content. I also change things up a little because I am so tired of dehydrated meals and oatmeal. From the store, we head to Hillary's home where her husband and three boys are waiting for us.

A delicious meal is being cooked, and it's aromas fill the air of Hillary's house, causing me to salivate at the wonderful smell. I begin to take off my shoes and socks at the door, but my feet are caked with dirt, so I decide to keep them on so as not to shock anyone.

Since the meal isn't completely finished cooking, Hillary shows me to my room. I shower, making it my fifth one in thirty-two days. I take my time enjoying the warmth of the water and scrubbing away the grime between my fingernails and toenails. I am gentle with my back wounds as they have finally started to scab over.

I put in a load of laundry and wash away the soap used by the trail angel and all the itchiness that went along with it. I then return to the dining room. Hillary's husband and three kids join us at the table. The smell is even better the closer I get to the meal that Hillary perfectly laid out before us. As Hillary removes the lid, I am taken back at how delicious and amazing everything looks. The meal is Green Chile Chicken with rice and corn. She also has placed a big glass of Dr. Pepper next to my plate. Hillary tells me she loaded my meal up with cream cheese to make it extra fattening, and we both giggle. I really do need to fatten up. I demolish everything on my plate and help myself to another serving. I don't leave the table until I feel like my stomach is about to explode. It is the first home-cooked meal I have eaten in over a month. It tastes amazing! When I return to my room, my body melts onto the bed, turning into a lump of Jell-O. I let out a silent *ahh*. I massage my feet and notice both heels are numb, especially my left one. It is a weird sensation to be numb and achy at the same time.

CHAPTER 40

August 5 - 8:10 a.m.

35.9 miles / 3,296 feet

12 hours, 57 minutes

"You have to get up every morning
and tell yourself, 'I can do this!'"

-Julie Johnston

BY SIX THE NEXT MORNING, I am ready to leave Hillary's house. She read my post on Instagram about my struggle with losing my spork and plastic utensils breaking on me. She gives me a titanium spork as I head out the door. Her husband Logan gives me a ride back. Before reaching the trailhead, we grab breakfast at McDonald's and make a quick stop at a gas station, where I buy a can of tobacco. I will use it as an offering to show respect for the land, my ancestors, and the creator. In the Blackfeet Culture, tobacco has always been a sacred plant offered when asking for help or showing gratitude before receiving a gift.

As I begin walking, my heels still feel numb. Weeks of hiking have taken a toll on them. I know I could use some new shoes. The rugged terrain has beaten them up a lot quicker than expected. Sadly, it won't be for another 400 miles before I will receive a new pair. My left shoulder also feels stiff. I think it is higher than the right causing me to carry most of the pack weight on the left shoulder. As I continue trekking on, I find it easy to fixate on all of my aches and pains without outside distractions. I come across two hikers who go by the names of Caveman and Iceman and quickly forget about everything hurting. The cleanliness of their appearance solidifies my assumptions that they, too, just came from town or are only backpacking for a few days.

Looking off into the distance, I see the sky has turned dark and gray. I can tell it is raining over there and begin to hear the thunder coming from its location. Hillary messages me to check if I am okay. The storm had brought thunder and hail to where they had dropped me off earlier. I am just enough ahead of the storm to where it doesn't affect me. The only thing I have to endure is a slight temperature drop that feels amazing as the clouds block the sun.

The sun is beginning to set a lot sooner than when I first hit the trail. I stay for a few moments thinking the sunrise must be spectacular. By evening, I camp out at mile 929 on the windy ridge.

CALIFORNIA

"All these storms falling upon us are signs that the weather will soon clear and that things will go well for us, for neither good nor bad can last forever."

-Don Quixote

CHAPTER 41

DAY 34 FEMALE FKT ATTEMPT

August 6 - 6:35 a.m.

39.7 miles / 7,556 feet

14 hours, 32 minutes

"She stood there bright as the sun
on that California coast."

-Bob Seger

I SPEND MOST OF THE DAY CLIMBING until I reach the clouds. It is such an amazing feeling to be so high up in the sky. Flowers paint both sides of the trail with their pink, purple, and yellow shades. There are a lot of bees feasting away on them, reminding me of when I was stung in Washington. I quickly roll my pant legs down to prevent a repeat. Someone has also taken advantage of the beautiful flowers creating a "1700!" mile marker on the dirt with them. The trail is so lovely and lush here. The ground is soft as though my feet respond with an "ooh" and "ahh" with every step.

I reach the Oregon/California boundary marker by six-thirty. It also has mileage engraved onto it, stating that Mexico is only a whopping 1,694 miles away, whereas Canada is 958 miles from here. Next to the sign is the trail register box. I open the metal lid and begin to read what others have written. Wildcats' entry catches my eye first, writing, "My feet hurt... good job, everyone!" This statement couldn't be more relatable. No matter how many miles I have hiked, my feet hurt by the end of the day. I grab one of the pens inside the box and begin to make my own entry. I write just below Wildcats, "Isht' Putaki - Flys High SOBO. ONTO CALI, my home for the next forever days - Wapato, WA." Wapato, Washington, was where I was raised and graduated high school. It's a small town, mostly made up of agricultural workers. Once I finish writing my entry, I close up the box and begin the California section.

The evening brings dense fog, reminding me of the fake stuff used for Halloween. I turn my headlamp on the dimmest setting. The high beam really brings out the fog, making it a lot more challenging to see what's ahead.

CHAPTER 42

August 7 - 6:26 a.m.

30 miles / 3,449 feet

10 hours, 20 minutes

"The wings of hope carry us, soaring high above the driving winds of life."

-Anna Jacob

I HAVE BEEN TAKING PHOTOS OF MY FACE EVERY DAY since the start of the trail. It is interesting to see the differences in my appearance as I scroll through them. The first few days on the PCT, I look refreshed, for the most part. My cheeks are a lot rounder. I can tell when I didn't get enough sleep from the night before. There are dark circles under my eyes, yet I am smiling in almost all of them. I really am happy to be out here. The experience far outweighs the physical suffering aspects. I snap a photo of my face, staring at the results for a few moments. My photo reminds me of a wild woman. There's dirt smudged across my cheeks. I haven't shaved my legs or plucked my eyebrows in weeks, and it shows. I am starting to form a unibrow. My hat and neck gaiter hide my crazy hairdo. Although I look like a hot mess, it is freeing not to care so much about my appearance. I have no one to impress but myself.

I am full of extra energy today, knowing that my mother has the weekend off to take a mini road trip to see me, and she will be bringing my kids with her. I asked my sister if she could pick up a new pair of trail shoes and send them with our mom. My feet would really appreciate it.

The hike into Seiad Valley is extremely hot and provides minimal shade. I cross paths with two hikers, Struggles and Charcoal. They are both sitting under some bushes hiding from the sun. They are an older couple accomplishing the trail post-retirement. Even though it is hot and water has been scarce, they still offer me theirs. I don't take any and thank them for their generosity. I only have five miles left before reaching the town, and it is all downhill from here.

When I reach Seiad Valley, I make my first stop at Wild-wood Tavern and Lodge. The lodge and hostess, Rachel, are excellent. She has created a nice little getaway for hikers and people passing through. There is a small store inside, Wi-Fi, a place to recharge electronics, and a bar. If you wanted, you could stay for the night to shower and do laundry. It is the perfect place to re-energize. I don't buy much when I enter: just a soda and a pint of mint chocolate chip ice cream. Rachel tells me the tavern has prepared a wonderful meal for dinner should I decide to stay. I really want to but also need to make it to my resupply box the store a half-mile away has stored for me. I thank her for the fantastic ice cream and soda, then head out the door.

I stop at the grocery store and pick up my resupply. I also buy ice-cold water and an apple. Fresh fruit is something I wish I had more of on my hike. There is no cell phone service in town, but I use the store's Wi-Fi to call my mom. She is still two hours away. I take the time to book the nearest available hotel room, which is twenty minutes away.

I walk over to the benches located near the store and take a seat. I set my hiking pack on the chair next to me and begin to eat away at my apple. There are a group of bikers sitting at the table across from me. They look exactly like what you would imagine bikers should look like. They are all wearing leather with their Harleys parked nearby. I comment on how amazing their bikes look and that I haven't ridden one in almost ten years. They begin to chat with me, and I tell them a little about the trail. They all agree that biking seems like an easier option, and we all laugh. Before leaving, they offer me a beer and wish me luck on my journey.

When my mom and kids arrive, we order pizza for dinner and stop at a gas station for snacks. As we sit around in the motel room, enjoying each other's company, I re-pack my hiking bag. I stuff it with my resupply items. My mother gives me my new shoes from Glenna. I don't know what it is about having a fresh pair of shoes, but my mood immediately improves. I know my feet will be happy tomorrow. I turn to my mom and say, "You know the saying, happy wife, happy life?"

She gives me a hesitant, "Yeah."

"Well it also holds true to feet," I say. "Happy feet keep me upbeat."

She laughs, saying, "That was horrible, Jess."

"I know, I just couldn't think of very many things that rhyme with feet or foot, but it is 100 percent true."

CHAPTER 43

August 8 - 10:32 a.m.

26.4 miles / 6,522 feet

10 hours, 56 minutes

"Everything can change in an instant. Everything. And then there is only before and after."

-Phyllis Reynolds Naylor

WE MAKE THE TWENTY-MINUTE DRIVE back to Seiad Valley. The first few miles out of town are along a paved road. My kids take turns hiking a mile, one at a time with me, as my mom follows in her vehicle. It is nice to get some alone time with each of them. There are berries all along the trail. We each stop to enjoy a few along the way until we reach mile 1,000.

No signs or big congratulatory markers celebrate this momentous occasion because hiking southbound is not the usual direction people go. Even the trail markers are all marked for northbound travel. To highlight the experience, we stop at the 1,000-mile point and take a few family photos. It is blazingly hot out, but my kids are troopers, just happy to hike. They hardly complain at all. When we finally reach the trailhead, we eat peanut butter sandwiches together. My kids get in the car but don't want me to leave. They ask Grandma if they can stay to hike with me for a little longer. She agrees. My mom and kids get out of the car and join me until the trail turns steep. It is always so difficult to say goodbye. We all hug and kiss each other, continuing to watch one another head off in different directions. I wave my final goodbye as I turn the corner, and soon they are no longer in sight.

It is a quiet hike up as I begin losing myself in thought. My mind wanders towards my kids. I think about their different personalities and spunky attitudes. My oldest son, Tennessee, is very sweet and kind. He is always making sure I am okay and watching out for his sisters. I always get compliments about his behavior and kindness towards others. He is a wonderful big brother. He loves to watch football with his dad and enjoys gaming on his console like most kids his age. My middle daughter is almost an exact replica of me. She is very mischievous and energetic. She likes to run and climb. She is a free spirit. Unlike me, though, she has a green thumb and enjoys gardening. Our youngest daughter is our cuddle monster. She is also our power hiker and would walk forever if you let her. Out of all three kids, she enjoys cooking and singing the most. She has even created a few of her own recipes and songs. I miss them already.

Since the moment we parted, I have been climbing while enjoying the peacefulness of this segment. I only pass two hikers on the way up. I don't think trail maintenance has been out here in a while, and I find myself bushwhacking every few feet. The bushes' long, pointy branches and leaves scrape against my bare legs, leaving scratches on my skin. After one digs into my thigh, drawing blood, I finally give in and reluctantly put my hiking pants back on. The heat is more comfortable with them off, but the open wounds on my legs are reason enough to suffer the added warmth. As I make my way closer to the top of the climb, weaving in and out of shrubs becomes minimal until I no longer have to fight my way out. I welcome the cool breeze, take off my hat, and let the wind cool off my head.

As though the trees agree, they squeak and moan as they sway in the wind. Then, out of nowhere, I hear the sound of one breaking off and falling in the distance, heightening my sense of awareness. Not too long after, I hear another tree mimicking the same noise, only this time it is coming from directly in front of me. I immediately stop as I watch the top half of a tree twenty feet away begin to break away from its base. But, I am ready. I instantly squat halfway towards the ground, ready to jump out of the way should it fall in my direction. Thankfully, gravity is on my side. The tree starts falling to the right of the trail towards the base of the mountain. A loud thump echoes in the woods as it lands. I pause for a minute in shock. I can't believe that just happened. I look around, hoping someone else just witnessed what I saw, but I am still alone. It is just me and the tree. I grab my can of tobacco and offer it to Mother Nature. I lay it at the base of the broken tree and thank it for not crushing me. At the time the tree had fallen, I wasn't scared. Maybe a part of my senses has become numb to what I should be feeling.

Maybe I just knew I would be okay. I also didn't have time to think about being afraid, but now I am leery and more aware of what a tree can do. I find myself looking at every tree I pass, wondering if it will break, too.

When I finally reach the top and am far away from the falling tree, my jaw drops open. "Wow! Just wow!" I continue to repeat. Most sunrises have left me awe-struck, but this is by far the best one yet. I feel like I have no choice but to stop, sit down, and take in every ounce of it. The vibrant sun looks like fire has let loose in the sky while creating a silhouette of mountain ranges in the distance. After a few minutes of *oohing* and *aahing*, I get up and continue on the trail.

I push on with the plans of meeting up with another ultra runner I know by evening. He has agreed to join me for thirty trail miles, a welcomed change of pace. I hike a few hours after sunset but don't make it to where we had hoped to link up. My headlamp catches tiny scorpions running away from its light. I am careful when setting up my tent, avoiding the possibility of being pinched by one. It isn't until I am in my tent almost asleep when I realize that I just checked off another bucket list item today: "See a falling tree." I could have done without the close call, though.

CHAPTER 44

DAY 37 FEMALE FKT ATTEMPT

August 9 - 5:16 a.m.

40 miles / 7,566 feet

16 hours, 4 minutes

"How glorious a greeting the sun gives the mountains."

-John Muir

I DIDN'T HEAR BACK from my trail-running friend Mica once I left Seiad Valley yesterday. But, I haven't had much for cell service either. This morning is no different. I wake up to the wind pushing against my tent. It is a little before five. If I leave now, maybe I can link up with him early. That is if he did sleep on the trail last night as planned. I am packed up and ready to go by 5:16 a.m. It is still dark out. The sky is clear, and the stars shine bright. I almost don't want the sun to awaken from its slumber. I am not even a mile into my hike before seeing two sets of lights heading in my direction. Eventually, the lights and I link up. The headlamps are from two hunters, Dillon and Michael. They are both big in size, at least six feet tall, and carrying similar hunting backpacks. They are brothers scouting out the area in search of deer and bears. We swap a few hunting stories and talk about different types of game we have both eaten. Thanks to my husband's Oryx hunt, I can one up them. I tell them I haven't seen any bears in the area, and unlike them, I am glad I haven't.

The sunrise mixes with splashes of orange and pink. I stop and absorb the beauty. I have yet to grow tired of watching it rise and set. Not long after, I pass a campsite with two tents still set up from the night. A few feet in front of them and slightly off the trail is someone sleeping in a bivy sack. A bivy sack is basically a waterproof sleeping bag. Thus far, I have seen a few hikers who have spent the night tucked inside of one, so I don't think much of it. Only that, I enjoy the tent life too much.

As I make my way past this bivy person, his head pops out. "Are you Jessica?" he asks.

"Yes, I am," I respond. "Hi, Mica." He tells me he slept on the trail all night, knowing that I would soon be passing. We seemed only to miss each other by a few miles. I am glad we manage to link up here. Although I have never had a problem running or hiking alone, hiking with Mica is a nice change of pace. Mica is small in stature and must be no more than five-foot-five. He is only carrying a running vest but somehow managed to fit all of his backpacking gear inside of it. Once he is packed up and ready to go, he shares that he was pretty freaked out last night. He saw a bobcat walk right past him towards the water. He sat still and watched it drink to make sure it left him alone. The bobcat walked back towards him and disappeared into the mountain, but he still had a fitful night of sleep.

It is a magical day on the trail. What an amazing area. This is my favorite section in California thus far. The trail is very mountainous, with no mosquitos, many lakes, and different shades of rock. We are so high up that the silhouette of mountains never ends.

Mica and I spend the day talking about our families and the races we have competed in over the years. I also share a few stories of my journey so far. Stories like having to self-arrest in Washington and getting sick in Oregon. I tell him that, so far, the trail has been excellent minus a few mishaps, and hopefully, California will be a lot kinder.

With only a few miles left before reaching Mica's truck, I secretly grab a pinch of tobacco from my pocket. I say a prayer of being thankful for today and ask the creator, Mother Earth, and my ancestors to protect and bless Mica once we head our separate ways. Then, when Mica is not looking, I quickly poke a hole into the dirt and gently place the tobacco into it as an offering.

When we've gone thirty-one miles, we see his truck parked at the trailhead with a cooler full of ice-cold orange soda. He pops two bottles open. We sit there enjoying the sugars and refreshing taste of soda. He also has two containers of quinoa and pasta. We begin pigging out, devouring everything. Before leaving, he heats some water and pours it into a dehydrated meal. He tells me to take it, along with some bread for dinner. I reply with, "Really? That is so awesome of you. Thank you!"

Mica agrees to hike two more miles with me before turning back. We make the climb up and away from the road. I share my bucket list with him. I tell him I don't have very many items on my list but have enjoyed trying to check them off. He asks which ones I have left. I say, "You know, I have hiked many nights on the trail. In fact, I love hiking at night and seeing the twinkling of the stars. But I have yet to see a shooting star."

He responds in disbelief. "How can that be possible?"

"I don't know. Maybe it's because I am so focused on the ground most of the time or find myself amongst the trees. I have no clue. I've looked up and stared at the sky almost every night and still have yet to see one." As we part ways, he tells me he hopes I can check off my last two bucket list items.

Despite being a Washington native, this part of the PCT has been my favorite place to hike so far. The sunsets in California are one-of-a-kind. They are full of fire, far superior to that of Washington or Oregon.

CHAPTER 45

DAY 38 FEMALE FKT ATTEMPT

August 10 - 6:28 a.m.

40 miles / 5,869 feet

15 hours, 2 minutes

"Forget about your worries and your strife."

-Baloo, *The Jungle Book*

I SPEND MY MORNING IN THE WOODS. The moss on the trees is bright green and fuzzy, just like the Grinch from the Dr. Seuss books. I've probably passed thousands of them before deciding to stop and touch one. The moss feels soft, reminding me of a kitchen sponge. There seems to be an abundance of it.

By evening, the color of the sky shifts from bright blue to a hazy orange. There is a lot of smoke coming from the distance, blocking the sun. The smell of smoke has made its way towards me. I speak with a few north bounders regarding what appears to be a fire off in the distance. They inform me that once I am past this section and turn the corner, I will begin to make my way far from it. I also share that I haven't seen any smoke near the trail until today. I message my brother for an update. I want to make sure I am out of harm's way and figure out if it has been contained. He replies minutes later and let's me know the fire is not near the trail and is under control. I thank him and continue hiking.

Five miles before reaching camp, I see three black bears, a mama and two cubs. They hear me well before I see them. I only notice where they are because they have started to run away. I continue walking as though nothing has happened.

My left foot and both heels continue to be bothersome. Both heels are numb and achy. I have been using the same style of shoes since the start of my hike. The same style I have been using for the past two years. The same type I have also used for all of my 200-mile races. It is too late to try and change them out. Although my heels are numb, I haven't had to deal with many blisters. I will just keep what I have. It's not like I have another choice anyway.

When I make it to camp, there are already two hikers set up for the evening. We chat for a few minutes while I put up my tent. I learn they are from Europe, heading northbound. Once I am inside my tent, their sleeping pads are loud. Every time one of them moves it creates a loud noise making it really difficult to fall asleep.

CHAPTER 46

DAY 39 FEMALE FKT ATTEMPT

August 11 - 5:04 a.m.

45 miles / 4,006 feet

15 hours, 56 minutes

"It is in the shade that you look up at
a tree and appreciate its effort."

-Matshona Dhliwayo

THE COUPLE MOVING AROUND ALL NIGHT also wakes me from sleep early. I give in and get an early start. Hopefully, I can bank some miles today despite how hot it is outside already. I notice small water blisters forming on my arms from the heat. They are tiny and not painful. I put extra sunscreen on, popping the few I have, even though I know I shouldn't.

I grab my bottle from the side of my pack and reach down into the stream to fill it up, capping it off with my water filter. A half-mile later, I am pretty thirsty. I reach back for it and begin to filter the water into my clean bottle. When I am halfway finished with filtering the water, I catch something swimming inside the bottle. I bring the bottle up closer to get a better look. Inside, there is a bug swimming around. I can't believe I almost filtered my entire bottle without noticing. I leave the remaining water inside and deem this swimming bug as my new pet, Pepé. I carry Pepé for the next four miles until I can place him safely back into a stream.

It is scorching today. My weather application tells me it is already 94 degrees outside and rising. My heart sinks, learning that the rest of the week will be well above 100 degrees. I take a rest at mile 1,125.1 next to White Ridge Spring. I splash water onto my face and neck, doing my best to cool off. Another hiker heading northbound is also seated near the area. He is tall, skinny, and looks to be in his late twenties. He is wearing a brimmed hat, and dust and sweat stains cover his clothes. I must look depleted because he offers me some of his food. I decline, telling him that I have a couple of days supply left and will be getting resupply in two days. He looks at me with a confused expression doubting my ability to make the 110 miles within that time frame. As I refill my water bottles, I thank him for offering me some food, get up, and continue my hot and cumbersome hike.

The hike to Castle Crags is rocky with minimal shade. Mount Shasta overpowers its craggy peaks. I go through my water supply fast. It is difficult to fathom that just a month ago, I was deep in snow. When I finally reach the top, it is a long way down, and I am all out of water. My mouth is dry. It is so hot outside that I can't even be cooled off by my own sweat. The heat takes it away before giving it a chance.

I begin to miss trail running. I try my best to run, but every step is a blow to my ego. Running is pointless. It hurts too much and isn't any faster than briskly walking.

Adding to the frustration, the gnats have also come out to play. No matter how many times I swat at them, they don't go away. I use my mosquito head net to keep them from sticking to my sweaty face and out of my mouth and nose.

I make it to a water source. It does not reach the trail but fizzles out a little way up. I follow the small path created by dozens of hikers walking up to find a spot to collect this precious resource. I stop once I see water. I grab a giant leaf and place the big part of it at the base of where it's trickling. I create a spout with the smaller end of the leaf, placing it at the opening of my bottle. The water slowly drips inside. I wait for over ten minutes for it to fill. I chug the entire bottle as though it is my last. I refill half of another bottle, but it is taking far too long, and I am anxious to make it to camp already. Instead of waiting to fill my bottle entirely, I continue hiking.

I hike until I reach a flowing water source to set up camp. When I crawl inside my tent, a stink bug has hunkered down for the night on my hiking pack. I open my tent to let it outside, but it flies back in, emitting a foul odor everywhere. Every time I reach for it, it lets out more stink. I am finally able to grab it with my hands and toss it out. Now, my hand and pack smell so rank. Just when I thought I couldn't smell any worse, this stink bug proves me wrong. I try to get rid of the smell with hand sanitizer. It helps a little, but the scent still stains my hiking pack.

CHAPTER 47

DAY 40 FEMALE FKT ATTEMPT

August 12 - 7:10 a.m.

37.5 miles / 5,702 feet

14 hours, 15 minutes

"Nothing brings to life again a
forgotten memory like fragrance."
-Christopher Poindexter

I WAKE UP TO THE LINGERING ODOR of the stink bug. I walk to the nearby stream and scrub my hands and pack, trying to get rid of the smell. I sit on a boulder with my feet submerged hoping that the cold water will wake my achy, numb heels. I also wash my socks, shirt, and underwear in the stream. When I return to my tent, I realize the odor covers the entire inside. That stink bug definitely wanted to leave his mark and did a number on my gear.

I only have exactly one day's supply of food left and one day of hiking before my next resupply, which worries me a little. However, before settling into an afternoon of climbing, I come across a red cooler full of trail magic. Trail angel Kellyfish has left an entire stock of food. The box contains Nutrigrain bars, Gatorade, coconut water, and a single beer inside. I grab a couple of bars and coconut water, leaving a thank you note behind. Her trail magic makes me feel at ease and gives me a greater cushion for making it to my next supply point.

Before leaving, I take a photo of a long message Kellyfish has left. It reads:

"When we embark on the journey to follow our joy and fulfill our destiny, our constant traveling companion, our ego mind wants to know all the details ahead of time. Where exactly are we going? How long will it take? Will we be safe and comfortable? Will we enjoy ourselves? Will we succeed in creating our desired outcome? Yet life is uncertain and can't be controlled. The good news is, that while uncertainty can be unsettling, it's also the source of our greatest joy." -Deepak Shopra.

I think about this message for a long time. When all you have are hours to yourself, it is easy to focus on the simplest things. Yet, the message Kellyfish left holds many truths. The trail is an adventure in itself, and the wilderness does as it pleases. I became happier on the trail when I decided to let go of where I think I should be and instead enjoy where I have made it to so far.

By evening, I make it to a camp next to a privy. This one has several notes on the Guthook application warning hikers to beware of all the bats near the restroom. Excited to have an actual toilet to sit on, I enter, but cautiously. I turn my headlamp to the lowest light setting to not disturb the bats hanging around. The bats don't bother me, and I hunker down near the privy for the night. When I exit, I try to check off my bucket list item of seeing a shooting star. I stare at the sky for a while but see none.

I wake in the middle of the night to the sound of something moaning. It is not an animal or something lurking outside my tent this time. Instead, it is me. My achy feet throb so much I started moaning in my sleep. It is the first time I think I have ever done this. I massage them for a few minutes before falling back to sleep.

CHAPTER 48

August 13 - 7:07 a.m.

37.1 miles / 7,221 feet

14 hours, 19 minutes

"If you want to see a shooting star, you might
have to spend a lot of nights looking up."

-Cynthia Lewis

I THINK I JUST SAW THE MOST UNIQUE THINGS on the PCT yet. I cross paths with two thru-hikers heading northbound. One of the hikers has a fluffy orange cat packed on his back. I learn that the couple has carried the cat for most of their journey. The couple also gives me intel on the State Park in the direction I am heading. They tell me they were disappointed to learn that it was closed when they passed through, but it will be open when I pass by tomorrow. Like most hikers I have passed, we wish each other a safe and great journey, then head on our way.

A few hours have passed since I saw the cat hikers. I am wary of the area I am in now. There are tall bushes on both sides of the trail filled with berries. It's the perfect place for a bear to feast. I try to make as much noise as I can by randomly singing and talking aloud to myself. I eventually grow tired and begin to daydream as I walk. Minutes later, directly in front and to the right of me, something makes a loud huffing sound. Only, I can't see what it is because the bushes are in the way. I pause, then slowly begin to back away, listening intently while looking up and around. I don't see or hear anything run off, and I don't see anything in the trees. I continue to backtrack until I feel I am a safe distance back. I stand, waiting, looking on my map for a way around. It's impossible to hike farther left because too many shrubs block the path. My only option is to stay on the trail. I wait fifteen minutes before continuing on. This time I am louder. I start talking to what I think was a bear. I spout, "Hey, bear. Hey, bear. I don't mean any harm, just trying to pass through. Hey, bear. Hey, bear." When I am well past the area, I let out a deep breath. *Man, that was close.*

Tonight, the sky is incredibly clear. After setting up my tent, I turn off my headlamp, refusing to enter until I see a shooting star. Not even thirty seconds pass before a star zips across the sky, taking my wish along for the ride. I enter my sleeping quilt with a big smile on my face, content to have checked off another bucket list item.

CHAPTER 49

August 14 & 15 - 6:53 a.m.

42.3 miles / 4,304 feet

15 hours, 20 minutes

"I've got plenty of common sense,
I just choose to ignore it."

-Bill Waterson

TODAY HAS BEEN THE HOTTEST DAY on the PCT. I message my sister about how hot it has been, and she suggests that I split my day up. "Of course, what a brilliant idea," I respond. I look at my map. I should be able to reach Burney Falls State Park by noon. Splitting the day into an early and late trek will allow me to miss the hottest parts of the day, recharge my electronics, buy food, and rest.

I make it to the State Park by noon. I find a shaded picnic area with electrical outlets. I plug in all of my electronics and make a beeline to the store. With all the miles and time spent hiking, food has become an obsession. I think about different types of foods at least a hundred times a day. As I enter the store, it isn't easy to decide on only a few items. I end up exiting with an ice cream cone, nachos, a hot dog, chips, and carbonated water. I return to the picnic area, devour all my food, and pull out my sleep mat. I lay it across a picnic bench, trying my best to take a nap. I try getting comfortable, but too many people are making noise. By five in the evening, I am ready to begin hiking again.

I look at the weather on my phone. Today's high was 107 degrees Fahrenheit, and it is only supposed to get hotter for the next few days. Also, this section is entirely bare and dusty, making it hotter still. I am glad once the sun sets. The light soon vanishes, making it pitch black outside. I turn on my headlamp, ready for a long night of hiking.

The trail passes alongside the Crystal Lake Fish Hatchery. It is brightly lit, surrounded by a tall metal fence. The hatchery reminds me of my kids because, over the years, Tim and I have taken them to quite a few of them. I take out my phone to record it to show them later. As I press the record button, I hear a loud splash, and then a head pops out of the water. I squint my eyes as if trying to get a better look, then widen them in disbelief. It is a black bear, and he is not alone. He and his companions are helping themselves to an all-you-can-eat buffet inside the hatchery. Soon, all the bears are looking at me. I reach up and turn my headlamp to its brightest setting.

By now, all of the bears have begun to run away. I watch intently, trying to see where they go. I count five in total. I continue to proceed with caution, thankful that the trail turns to the right, up and away from the Crystal Lake Hatchery, but I am soon mistaken. The trail crosses the road and makes a sharp left in the direction of where I saw the bears run off to last. With my headlamp still on the highest light setting, I look back and forth on the trail ahead. I get several sets of eyes glowing back at me. They are directly on the trail. I back up slowly and take the far-left side of the road away from where the bears are standing. I keep my light on them the entire time until I turn the corner and they are no longer in sight.

I don't know what it is about this section of the trail. Maybe it's the fact that I came across bears or that there is a ton of bear scat everywhere, but it feels eerie. Like a million sets of eyes are constantly staring at me.

I cross a rusty bridge near the Hydro Electrical Plant, where I meet a wooden billboard. I make the mistake of reading it. Although I have heard everything on the sign before, it doesn't help improve how I am feeling now. The poster is full of warning signs. I read it aloud, responding to each warning.

"Number one: Beware of Bears!"

"Too late," I say.

"Number Two: You are in Mountain Lion Territory."

"Oh good," I respond sarcastically.

"Number Three: Don't Hike from Dawn to Dusk."

"That is exactly what I have been doing this entire hike."

"Number Four and Five: Don't Hike Alone and Don't Hike at Night.

"Seriously," I say.

Already spooked, I stop to change into pants and collect myself. Just as I begin to slide my feet into them, a giant bat flies directly in front of me, freaking me out even more. I take a few breaths and give myself a pep talk. "C'mon, Jess. You love night hiking. This is nothing." I say my Indian name a few times out loud for strength and courage, "Isht' Putaki. Isht' Putaki. You got this."

There are giant bushes everywhere. I start to blast music from my phone's speaker. I want anyone or anything around to know I am here. Whatever may be lurking around these bushes tonight should not only see me but hear me coming and hopefully run off. When I finally make it out of the shrubs and into an area I am comfortable with, I turn off the music on my phone, and I take an extra moment to look up at the stars. As I raise my head, two shooting stars race across the sky towards the bright orange crescent moon. I don't bother to make a wish. I already have everything I need.

I eventually make it to a camp area, and a few feet from the trail, I see a man cowboy camping. Cowboy camping is the lightest form of camping that includes the freedom from carrying a shelter or sleeping hammock. This man does not have a tent and has chosen to lie in his sleeping bag with his bald head popping out. After everything I experienced tonight, I wouldn't have the guts to sleep like that. I don't think I could ever leave myself so exposed to the elements and wildlife. At least not here. I leave this area and continue hiking for another six miles until I reach my planned site. It is three in the morning, and I let out a relieved and celebratory whisper of, "Woohoo," once I finally make it. Usually, my long-distance trail plans never work out, so I let myself enjoy this small victory.

CHAPTER 50

August 15 - 6:42 a.m.

27.5 miles / 3,038 feet

10 hours, 20 minutes

"Strength and growth come only through
continuous effort and struggle."

-Napoleon Hill

I WAKE EARLY TO THE VOICES of two older women and a teenager, camped not too far from me. I start to think about how many hours I just slept and calculate it at less than four. I have been far more sleep-deprived before. My first 200-mile race was in Washington State, called the Bigfoot 200. I had never done that distance before, so I was unfamiliar with how my body would react to the lack of sleep. For these types of races, there are sleep stations. It is up to the runner to decide how much or how little sleep they want. During that race, I was the second female to finish. I slept just three hours during that event. After completing two more 200-mile races the next two months, the following year, I participated in the Franklin Mountain 200 miler. During that race, I slept less than thirty minutes in seventy-one hours and won the female division. After thinking about how little sleep I have gotten in those previous events, I decided to just get up. Besides that, the warmth from the sun has already begun to make my tent feel like a sauna. I really should get going.

I chose this campsite because of the water tank placed here by a trail angel. Without it, hikers would have to carry water for over twenty miles before reaching another source. I am incredibly thankful for the tank because this section is by far the most grueling due to the heat and the scarcity of trees. Mica had warned me about this area known as Hat Creek. He urged me to try hiking most of it at night and make sure I have plenty of water. I was able to hike a good portion of it last night but still have a significant way to go. Running off a few hours of sleep, I chug one bottle of water, fill up three with water, and one with coffee. I know I need to knock out Hat Creek before the heat of the day.

It is only nine in the morning, and the sun is emitting an intense amount of heat. I feel like I am back in Iraq. I remember the feeling of getting off the airplane when we first arrived. It felt like a hairdryer blasting me in the face, turned on the highest and hottest setting. Only here, there is no breeze, only the magnified hot sun with its heat radiating off the rocks and ground.

I stop to change into shorts. As I reach into my pack for them, I take another look at my hands as I do each day. They look aged and weathered with dirt ingrained between the lines of my skin. My hardened skin is partially peeling from holding my trekking poles between my thumb and index finger. Dirt sticks underneath all of my nails. No matter how hard I try to clean out the grit, they are filled again by the end of the day. They are darker than usual from the sun beaming down on me. They look bruised and scabbed. I lather them with sunscreen and coat my arms just the same. It is boiling outside.

Just like my hands, Hat Creek is rough and rugged. There is minimal shade, and the water in my bottles has turned hot. Hiking in the heat of the day feels like I am running my first marathon in Iraq. A day had passed since returning from a mission. The gym was my healthy outlet. It was where I went to clear my mind and prepare for my next convoy. A friend and I were getting ready to tackle an upper body workout when a sign posted to the gym wall caught our attention. It was an announcement for a marathon. The race was to take place the following day at five in the morning. The route was a 26.2-mile loop around the base. As we read the sign, a Corporal approached us, stating that he had signed up for the race. My friend and I looked at each other, both thinking the same thing. I spoke first. With an enthusiastic and confident voice, I said, "Let's run it!"

My friend looked at me and responded with, "Okay, let's do this."

The Corporal immediately put us down, telling us, "I have been training for this, and you haven't. You guys are going to fail." His comments of discouragement made me want to prove him wrong. It lit a fire in me. I don't like people underestimating me. That afternoon, I did a little research on running marathons, learning that most athletes carry carbohydrate-rich energy gels. The job of the gel involves replenishing lost glycogen and calories lost during exercise. I was surprised to find our little store carried gels and bought two strawberry-flavored ones. As I exited the store, curiosity kept me from waiting until the next day to try one. The gel came in a small packet. I ripped it open and was surprised by the taste. It wasn't horrible, but it also wasn't great. It was sweet and shared the same texture as toothpaste.

When the next day arrived, I was nervous and had no idea what I was getting myself into with this marathon. We showed up early to the starting line with our headlamps on, eager to begin. The first half of the marathon passed with ease and was the furthest I had ever ran. There was only one aid station the entire route. The aid station was limited, only carrying bananas, Gatorade, and water. As my friend and I approached it, we saw the Corporal sitting on the ground with his shoes off. He told us that his feet are hurting too much, and he will stop at this mark. He told us we should do the same. We shook our heads no, took a few swigs of water, refilled the water bottles we had been carrying, and continued, more eager than before to finish.

After eighteen miles, we were suffering. There were no aid stations or water points since we left the halfway mark. Now boiling in the same manner as my PCT water bottles, our water was running low. We were down to our last few sips. There were no trees to shield us from the hot Iraq sun. The temperature on the pavement easily had to be in the 100s. Our legs started cramping, bringing our slow jog to a walk. The next few miles were painful. We were not prepared for the distance but kept moving. We knew that as long as we could walk, we could finish. We devised a plan of jogging for a few minutes then walking for a few minutes. This pace seemed to work, but we were running low on fumes. I still had my gel, though. At twenty-two miles, I take the hot gel out of my pocket. I finish half and give the other half to my friend. After a minute had passed, I could feel the gel working its wonderful magic as energy began to course throughout my body. I felt energized and ready to be done. We ended up finishing the race. I placed first female overall only because I was the only female to finish. I remember the feeling afterward. I felt incredibly sore but accomplished. I doubted I'd ever want to run a marathon again. We never heard back from the Corporal, but it didn't matter. His words pushed us to finish. So, in a way, I am glad he doubted us.

My first marathon in Iraq was challenging, but I managed to make it through. I continue to walk on the Hat Creek Rim trail all morning and afternoon. It is a dry and dusty field, but the reminder of my first marathon puts a smirk on my face. But just like that race, I have to keep moving forward.

There are a few trees in this area, but they don't provide enough shade or protection from the heat and the sun. Dirt covers my arms, legs, and face. It's difficult to drink hot water when you are burning up. My lack of sleep is intensified with the sun quickly zapping my energy, making me want to fall asleep. I drag on as though I am in a daze. I start to pray for strength and power to pull me through this tough section. Then, as though my prayers have been answered, I get a burst of energy and can pick up my pace.

I reach a metal gate where a trail registry stands. I open the metal lid to make a quick entry: "8/15/20 FLYS HIGH SOBO." I don't feel up to writing anything else. There are more trees in the area once I make it past the registry, but I don't stop to rest. My shoes are falling apart once again. The soles of both have begun to peel away from my shoe. They start catching on rocks until I stop and tear them off. The missing sole from my heels changes my gait, but I don't care. I am getting a new clean pair in town today.

The Pacific Crest Trail crosses paths with a trailhead easily accessible by car. There is a giant red fire truck parked inside its lot near a rustic pit toilet. One of the men inside the truck waves and says hello.

I respond, "Hi, how are you?"

The man replies, "Good and you?"

I say, "I am fine. It's really hot outside." He nods in agreement then offers me an ice-cold bottle of water. As he tosses one my way, I smile back, say a thank you, and continue hiking on. After drinking hot water all day, this bottle tastes beyond amazing. I drink the entire bottle in less than a minute.

I make it to town by one that afternoon. I have already hiked in the dead heat of the day and think about continuing, but I need to charge my electronics. I pick up my resupply from the Old Station Fill Up gas station then walk over to the cafe next door. As I begin to order, the cashier asks me if I am hiking the Pacific Crest Trail. I give her a nod.

She asks, "Are you hiking alone?"

I am hesitant to answer but respond with, "Yes, I am."

She says, "There are so many scary things in the woods that terrify me, like mountain lions and bears. You shouldn't be hiking by yourself." Completely thrown off by her comment, I don't quite know how to respond. I take a brief second to think about what she is saying and tell her I have been hiking solo for over thirty days and nothing has bothered me. I then give her my order and exit the building.

There aren't many places to sit since COVID-19 restricts indoor dining, making outdoor seating the only option. I score a small table that seats two right next to an outlet. As I wait for my food, another hiker walks up, searching for a place to sit. I offer her the chair next to me. I am actually excited to meet another female who is also hiking solo. We begin to chat. I introduce myself as Flys High, and learn that her trail name is Grit. We swap trail stories about our journeys so far and agree that cocoa and coffee are the best combination ever. I end up giving Grit a few packets of PERC Coffee before we part ways.

I walk towards the gas station again and notice a bench to place my resupply box on top and begin laying everything out. The first things I grab are my new pair of shoes and clean socks. The next thing I pull out is the dreaded bear canister. It's very bulky and weighs more than my bear bag. The following National Parks I will enter from here on out require a bear canister if you carry in food or anything that might attract bears. This includes my scented items, such as toothpaste and sunscreen. Without one, I would be breaking a federal regulation and have to pay a hefty fine. I continue rummaging through the box, sorting through my clean shirt, shorts, and food. I feel entirely overwhelmed thinking, *I have no idea where I am going to store everything.* Initially, I had planned to walk to the post office and mail off my excess items, but it's closed. While sorting through all of my things and deciding what to do with them, a truck pulls up. An older gentleman gets out and goes into the gas station. When he returns, we begin chatting about the trail. He offers me a giant peach. I can't resist fresh fruit since it's a rarity out on the PCT. I instantly start munching away while we continue talking.

Shortly after the man pulls out of the gas station, two white vans park in its place, and out steps a gentleman, two women, and a group of girls. The women approach me, and we begin talking while the rest of the troop enters the store. I learn that the troop is made up of all females. One of the troop leaders asks if I can speak with their scouts about the Pacific Crest Trail. When the girls return, I tell them they can ask me anything about the trail. It is a joy to talk with them because of how respectful and interested they seem. They ask me questions like how long the PCT is, what it's been like so far, and if I had anything scary happen to me. I tell them that the trail is 2,650 miles long, and it has been an amazing experience so far. I have learned a lot about myself. I also tell them about the bears feasting away at the fish hatchery. They get a kick out of this story. The girls are all extremely polite, and I only hope I can positively influence them. One of the troop leaders also volunteers to mail out my extra gear for me. How awesome is this!? I just met this group of strong females, and one of the leaders has agreed to mail out all of the things that were causing me stress and anxiety. I grab money from my pack and offer to cover the shipping fee, but the scout leader refuses it and tells me she will mail it for free. Once more, they also give me a ride back to the trailhead.

By evening, I enter Lassen Volcanic National Park. Although I am not thrilled about having to carry a bear canister, it is nice not having to tie it off to a tree. All I have to do is hike away from my tent and place it on the ground.

It's now the middle of the night, and I wake to the sound of two animals huffing near my tent. I yell out, "Helloooo!" and listen intently. In a little over a minute, I hear the sound of paws thundering away.

CHAPTER 51

August 16 - 6:16 a.m.

40 miles / 5,633 feet

14 hours, 18 minutes

"Everybody needs beauty. As well as bread,
places to play in and pray in, where nature
may heal and give strength to body and soul."
-John Muir

IN THE MORNING, I peer out of my tent and notice two sets of prints embedded in the dirt. I bend down and place my hand next to a large print. My hand is as big as the print. It definitely belongs to a bear. I pack up my things and am all too happy to make my way through Lassen Volcanic National Park, hopefully without any bear sightings.

The woods are silent this morning except for the sound of something hitting the ground in front of me. I stop and take a look until I find the source. It is a squirrel working intently towards collecting pine cones. He grabs a pine cone and then

271

tosses it to the forest floor to stash for later. It is something I have never seen before. He isn't even bothered that I am standing there watching. The trail leads directly under his tree. I am careful not to be hit by one of his falling food sources as I pass.

Still not recovered from the lack of sleep I've had these past few nights, my mind starts playing tricks on me. It is crazy how your mind begins to see things when you don't get enough sleep. I am all too familiar with this from my previous 200-mile races. I remember running the Franklins Mountain race for the first time and continuing to ask my friend Victoriano, who was pacing me, if a rock was in fact a rock and not something else I was imagining. So, as I am now walking through these woods, I think I see a black cat from the corner of my eye. When I turn to look at it, I realize it is just a burned log. Although I know it is a log, it really does look like a cat. I shake my head, telling myself to get it together but am soon back to seeing things. This time it is a woman with braided hair wearing a long, dark brown shawl. She sits directly on the path ahead of me but I know it's just a log. *You need to get some sleep*, I think to myself.

By afternoon, the wind picks up, and the sky turns overcast. I enter a burn area full of standing dead trees. I have already seen how powerful a falling tree is and don't want any to fall on me. I watch as the trees sway back and forth, waiting for one to fall over at any moment. I feel on edge as I watch my surroundings intently.

After yesterday's heat, I welcome the coolness. At least until I get a weather warning on my inReach. A storm is about to hit. I am not too far from Drakesbad Guest Ranch. According to my guide, they offer lunch between twelve and one. I am exactly in that window. I make the extra 0.4-mile hike to the ranch. The added mileage is well worth what I get in return. I have shelter from the storm, a place to charge my electronics, wonderful staff, and a delicious nacho lunch. When the storm passes, I leave the ranch and continue until I am near Boiling Springs Lake. The trail crosses so close to the lake, I can't help but take a few minutes to see it for myself. As I hike closer, the scent of the large sulfur spring becomes stronger, smelling like boiled eggs. The water is a milky blue color and gives off a good amount of steam.

A few miles past the spring, someone has posted a laminated black and white photo of John Muir to a tree. Under the photo is the date: (1838-1914). I know who this man is and have read several of his books. He was an advocate for the preservation of wilderness and is considered the father of National Parks. Muir is one of the many reasons I was able to hike through Lassen Volcanic National Park. Without him, the park may have never existed.

By evening, I find a nice campsite near Soldier Creek, near the base of my next 2,000-foot climb. I look at my phone, realizing that tomorrow I will be reaching an important milestone on the Pacific Crest Trail.

CHAPTER 52

August 17 - 6:35 a.m.

36.8 miles / 5,620 feet

14 hours, 52 minutes

"Nature, in her untamed state,
is savage and unrelenting."

-Fennel Hudson

AT 6:35 A.M., I finally make it out of camp. The sun is shining brightly through the trees, and it looks to be another gorgeous day. After two and a half hours of hiking, I begin to notice the sky shift. Off in the distance, I see dark and gloomy cloud cover. I turn my phone on to check for a weather update, but the internet is slow and impossible to load. I leave my phone on in hopes of receiving service. Maybe the weather report will chime in or I'll receive a message from my husband, kids, and family.

I usually turn my phone on once I reach a peak for the best reception, and I look forward to seeing my messages every day. It's as if I am playing satellite roulette. Sometimes my phone will ding, and other times I am not so lucky. Today I am close to a town and know that I have a good chance of getting a signal once I make it further up in elevation.

As I make my way closer towards the peak, my phone starts to ring. I pull it out of my pocket. It is my son's school. Usually, I would just let it go to voicemail, but the school year is about to start, so it must be important. "Hello, is this Mrs. Pekari?"

"Yes," I say.

"This is Tennessee's teacher from Jackson Elementary." I stop hiking, fearing I will lose the signal again. At this point, I am standing on a mountainside listening to her discussing how this year my kids will be taking courses online due to COVID-19. I tell her that his Grandma will be in charge of making sure his schoolwork gets completed. I inform her I am on the Pacific Crest Trail and won't return home until September. I let her know that his dad is deployed and give her my mother's contact information. Once we finish talking, I hang up the phone and continue.

It is nine in the morning, and the darkness of the sky is making its way closer toward me. I pull out my phone and try for a weather report again. Nothing. I turn on my Garmin inReach and search for a weather report. Still nothing. Moments later, my phone goes off with a weather warning: "Strong thunderstorms will affect portions of Northern California through 5:30 p.m...." The sky begins to grumble. *What should I do now?*

My phone chimes again. This time it is my husband. He could not have messaged at a more appropriate time. I tell him a storm is about to hit. I can hear thunder and have seen a few lightning strikes in the distance. He asks if I can get to an open area and wait it out. I am a quarter-mile from the peak.

I tell him, "NO! I am surrounded by trees."

He tells me to hike back down. I message, "I will do my best." I step off trail and begin to quickly move downhill in an attempt to distance myself from the peak as far as possible.

After a few minutes, I come to a halt. I find a place to hunker down and wait it out. I throw my trekking poles, which are basically aluminum lightning rods, off to the side and sit down. I should have listened to my gut telling me to turn around when I first noticed a change in the sky a few hours ago. But where would I have gone? If I had backtracked on the trail, I might still have been in the same situation I am in now.

The lightning and thunder continue to move closer. I begin counting. One-one thousand, two-one thousand, boom. One-one thousand, two-one, boom. Eventually, I don't even make it past one before the sky grumbles overhead, knocking at my soul.

The thunder and lightning remind me of a soldier I treated when I was on active duty. In preparing to go to Iraq, we were flown from Fort Bragg, North Carolina, to Fort Polk, Louisiana, for a field training exercise. My platoon was in charge of setting up and running a field hospital. The lightning in Louisiana was unlike anything I had ever experienced. At least until now. The amount of downpour it brought under our giant *M.A.S.H.*-looking tent was intense.

Our job was to find a solution for keeping our equipment out of the river during the storm. We ended up rearranging everything onto wooden crates. One afternoon, another lightning storm made its way towards us. Two other medics, a physician assistant, and I were on shift, waiting for the rush of rain the storm would bring. While we were making sure all of our electrical equipment was high off the ground, we heard someone yelling for a medic. We quickly grabbed a litter with the lightning overhead and ran over to the emergency. A soldier was lying on the ground, passed out. We learned that one of the lightning strikes hit his Humvee while he was leaning up against it. His hand was on the door when the lightning had struck, and it zapped him.

The lightning and thunder continued their dance overhead as we loaded the soldier onto the litter. We didn't have time to think about the weather and rushed him inside the medical tent. From there, we checked for entry and exit wounds but didn't find any. He woke up a few minutes later. We learned it was the second time this has happened to him. Although incredibly lucky, we still evacuated him to a greater level of care.

As the sky continues rumbling, I find myself fixating on negative thoughts. That soldier had been lucky. What would happen if lightning struck me, especially since I made the mistake of stepping off the trail in an attempt to make a beeline closer towards the base. I begin to have a difficult time trying to shake my thoughts of worst-case scenarios. I take out some tobacco to offer the creator. I ask for help. I pray the storm will not harm me, and I pray for safety. I pray for a clear and peaceful mind.

I shift my focus to the carpenter ants scattered all along the forest floor. They don't seem bothered by the lightning and thunder that has now made its way directly over us. Just then, lightning strikes to the right of me, followed by another strike to my left. I now think the teacher's phone call this morning may have just saved my life. If I had hiked just a few more minutes up the trail, I would be directly in the line of where that lightning had struck. If I were a few minutes behind, I would also be in the same situation.

The lightning is a reminder of how quickly the weather can turn, no matter how prepared you think you are. I can't believe this is happening. It all feels like a terrible nightmare that I am waiting to wake up from. I close my eyes as tight as I can and continue praying. The storm soon moves on, now only leaving drops of rain behind. I get up from where I am seated, grab my lightning rods, and hike back up to where I had left the trail. Within minutes I hike my way to the halfway marker trying to forget about everything that just happened. *This is it!* I am halfway finished. An immense amount of gratitude and accomplishment fills me. I drop to my knees, hugging the halfway marker as though it were my child. It is all downhill from here. *It can only get easier, right?*

I message my husband, mom, sister, and Rebecca. I let them know I have made it to the midpoint marker. I sit on the bench next to the stone pillar that highlights the halfway point and take a few minutes to soak it all in. I then reach down into the ammo can beside me and pull out the trail registry. I don't even know what to write. I try to come up with some cheesy quote or message to mark this extraordinary achievement, but my mind draws a blank. I end up writing what I have been telling myself almost every day on the PCT, "One more mile is one less mile."

I follow it up with, "Halfway there, SOBO BABY! -Flys High Woman." I close up the book, place it back near the pillar, and continue on the trail.

In less than a mile, I cross paths with another hiker who introduces himself as Crazy Legs. He is a bit taller than me and seems to be around the same age. His appearance looks as rough, rugged, and skinny as mine. We talk about how intense and scary the lightning storm had been. He was crouched on Butt Mountain and was only a quarter-mile away when lightning struck a nearby tree. He starts to joke that dying on Butt Mountain would have been an embarrassing way to go out, and I laugh in agreement. Before setting off on our separate ways, he tells me to look out for the struck tree because it isn't too far from where we are now.

It isn't long before I am standing directly in front of the struck tree with my mouth wide open in amazement. It is something I had never seen before. The scar spans from the very top where the lightning struck to the bottom. The smell of freshly cut wood fills the air, and chunks of the tree lay scattered across the ground. I pick up a piece, rolling it between my fingers. Then, as though the tree can hear me, I tell it I am sorry it was struck.

Once I make it off of Butt Mountain, I follow the ridgeline but am uneasy about the dark clouds accumulating in the distance. Normally I love hiking atop mountains and along their peaks and ridges, but today is different. I can't wait to get off of this mountain and into a lower altitude. I thought this morning's storm was done and over with, but I was wrong. Another wave of thunder and lightning make their way towards me. I want to keep hiking. I don't want to stop. I just want to be off of this ridge and into a safer location.

I pick up my pace but soon come to a stop. Something inside tells me not to go any further, that I should hunker down and just wait it out. I am glad I listen to my intuition because less than a quarter of a mile directly in front of me, flashes of lightning fill the air. If I had kept hiking, I would be exactly where they are striking. My heart rate begins to beat faster as the raging rain comes down and the sky rumbles. *Please, not again,* I say to myself, realizing this is the most afraid I have been since being on the trail. I would rather be back on the side of a mountain and covered in snow. Unfortunately, I can't control the weather, which brings me back to my days as a medic.

I don't like feeling helpless and attempt to focus on something else. I reach into my hiking pack for rain gear. The temperature has plummeted. I put my layers on and grab a pinch of tobacco and begin to pray. Within seconds, calmness courses through my body, and I know I will be okay. I know this too shall pass. A few more flashes of lightning occur before the storm moves on. The sun comes out, and the temperature warms back up. I take off my layers of warmth and stuff them back into my pack. I can only hope this is the last of it.

The storms shatter my plans for making it into Belden tonight. It has taken me eight hours to hike eighteen miles. Like most plans I have made while being out here, something always gets in the way. I have learned to just roll with the punches and keep chugging along. Eventually, I will get to where I need to be.

I am surprised to come across other hikers heading north-bound. I don't stop to chat with any of them. I just want to make it off of this ridgeline before I meet another wave of lightning. I can only begin to wonder what their experience had been like with the storms.

I make it to Cold Spring, mile 1,347.7. I refill my water bottles after having a twenty-mile water carry. The spring is near Humbug Summit Road. I am surprised to see vehicles up here. While filling, a truck parks nearby, and a couple exits the vehicle. They are much older than I am and have a dog in tow. The dog jumps out, wagging its tail excitedly, and makes its way towards me. The couple follows, and we begin to chat. I learn that they have been driving around checking out trailheads, trying to find an easy route. The gentleman is planning to do a few day hikes with a friend. The wife would drop them off at a trailhead and meet them further along the way. He then looks down at my hiking pack propped up near the spring and asks me how much it weighs. With a big smile on my face, I tell him, "I really don't have a clue, but you are more than welcome to lift it." He walks over, grabs one of the straps, raises my pack a few feet off of the ground, then quickly sets it down.

He then replies, "Whoa, this is why I day hike. I can't do that. I am too old. I don't have good knees." I don't respond but give him an understanding smile.

The couple continues discussing my hiking gear and filtration system. They also ask about my dehydrated meal of spaghetti and closely watch as I pour water on it. I tell them I don't carry a stove and cold soak my meals. After pouring the water into my meal bags, I have to let my food hydrate for a while before eating. Otherwise, my food will be crispy. I also hold up my water filter so they can get a good glimpse at it. With the storms that I have had to endure today and the possibility of more, a part of me wants to ask them for a hitch into town. But, of course, I don't, because I doubt anyone would be willing to give me a ride back to this exact location.

After leaving them, I hike a few more miles near the crest of a ridge. I turn my phone back on and am happy to have phone service once again. This time I call my mom. She informs me that she will be heading to Colorado tomorrow so the kids can pick up their school computers, books, and supplies. She also mentions she and my kids would like to meet me on the trail one last time before they head back to school, which surprises and excites me. I thought I wasn't going to see them again until after I finished the PCT. I look at the map on my phone to find a suitable meeting place. The closest road that allows me some hiking miles and time to hang with my kids is near Buck Lake, roughly fifty-four miles away.

By sunset, I make it out of the Cascade Range and enter the Sierra Nevada. It's hard to believe that "Sierra Nevada" translates to "snowy mountains" when I will be hiking them in the summer. I am sure the winter months hold meaning to the words, "Sierra Nevada," but for now, I will have to endure them in the heat.

CHAPTER 53

DAY 46 FEMALE FKT ATTEMPT

August 18 - 6:08 a.m.

27.5 miles / 6,325 feet

12 hours, 7 minutes

"Ignorance of impending evil is far better than a knowledge of its approach."

-Marcus Tullius Cicero

IN ONLY A FEW SHORT MILES, I cross over a bridge and make it into Belden. The town is near the North Fork Feather River. A small grocery store in Belden has benches outside where I can charge my electronics. The town is tiny, with only a few buildings around. When I make it to the store, it is eight in the morning, but it doesn't open until eleven. And there is no cellphone service. I only have twenty-four miles to make it to the meet-up location with my mom. I am so excited to see my kids today. While waiting and charging, a lady who lives next door begins to walk nearby. I greet her and ask if there is any Wi-Fi. She gives me the password, and I call my mom. Unfortunately, she won't be able to meet until ten that night. Soon an older gentleman passes by, and I begin chatting with him and learn that he is the store's owner. He graciously opens his store for me so that I can buy a few snacks.

Before leaving Beldin, I make one last stop at the privy. The privy is very dark inside with mouse poop scattered around the floor. I soon meet the culprit. There is a tiny white mouse perched atop some wire looking at me from a window. I don't shoo it away, but I finish what I am doing, and as quickly as possible, I shoot out the door.

It is a long, hot, and uphill climb out of Beldin. I stop to catch my breath and watch a helicopter hover over the river below. It fills up its enormous water bucket and flies off. Another quarter of a mile up the mountain, another helicopter appears. It too hovers over the river and refills its bucket. I see the helicopters come and go until I finally make it up and over this section. It is really scorching today. Someone on the Guthook application warns of poison oak and rattlesnakes all along the trail. Although rattlesnakes do worry me, I am not bothered by the poison oak. I have been brushing up against it for days while wearing shorts and am fortunate enough not to be allergic.

The view from the top is hazy and must be the reason for all of the helicopters filling up their water buckets. There must be a fire nearby. I try to find the source, but there is no clue where it starts. I can only figure out a general direction from where the smoke billows.

With hours left to go before my mom is set to arrive, I take my time. I sit on the rocky trail above two bodies of water. I have service here, so I call my sister, and she chats with me until I am finished eating. I begin to describe the area to her.

There are two tiny, dark green lakes below me, surrounded by slabs of boulders and shrubs. The sky is hazy, but the view from up here is one-of-a-kind. There are so many bright green, moss-lined trees around me. There is a dead tree behind me, but what's cool is although it is dead, there is new life growing on top of it. Chicken of the woods covers it. My sister laughs and says, "You must be hungry, chicken? Really?"

I laugh back. "No, not real chicken but mushrooms that are called 'chicken of the woods.'"

"Ahh," she says. I tell her they remind me of the orange spray foam you use for insulating a house. We talk for almost twenty minutes before I tell her I need to go.

By dinner time, I begin hiking down towards Buck Lake. There is smoke off in the distance that makes me feel uneasy. I grab my phone to make sure the trail does not lead towards it. *Oh no, please no.* My heart drops as I hold my phone up in the direction of the smoke. The trail seems to be in the direct line of where it is at. I try to be optimistic and talk myself into remaining positive. *The trail probably curves to the left. I am sure the PCT doesn't go anywhere near it.*

In the back of my mind, I want everything I am saying to be true. It has to be, but within a mile, everything comes to an end. I cross the road and look for where the trail connects. The wooden PCT sign where the trail picks back up has an orange ribbon hanging from it. Posted is a laminated piece of computer paper. I read the paper slowly, letting every single word sink in my head. On top, there is a Forest Service Department of Agriculture emblem. Below the emblem and in capital letters reads, "PACIFIC CREST TRAIL CLOSED DUE TO FIRES. QUESTIONS REGARDING INCIDENT PLEASE CALL THE FOREST SERVICE." I am in disbelief. This can't be real. I read it again and again. Part of me wants to be rebellious and keep hiking. There is no one around to see me. Nothing blocks my way. No fence, no gate, no one. There is only this sign, a regular white piece of paper.

I look on my app to find another way around. There is nothing but the road, which adds an absurd amount of additional mileage. I focus on the sign and see footsteps that also shared my same thoughts. But these steps circle back as if they too come to accept the reality of the situation. I'm heartbroken. I wish I could continue, but I know the damage a fire can do and how quickly it can move. The possibility of being burned to a crisp or the hefty fines for breaking the law and continuing on a closed trail is far beyond the boundaries I am willing to push.

So now what? Where do I go from here? I take a few deep breaths and turn around. I cross the road and begin to backtrack on the trail until I have cellphone service. It is almost dark out before I get a single bar. Even then, it cuts in and out of service. Finally, I can message my mom and give her a new pick-up location. I receive a message back on my inReach that she will not make it until two in the morning. I set up my tent directly on the trail, set the alarm, and fall asleep.

As soon as my alarm goes off, I peek my head out of the tent. The smoke has thickened. So much smoke fills the air. It's making me feel uneasy and all too happy my mother will arrive soon to rescue me once again. I don't bother placing all my items perfectly into my hiking pack. Instead, I quickly stuff everything inside and hike back down to the road. I wait, sitting next to the privy. Twenty-five minutes later, I see the dimmed headlights making their way through the smoke. My mom has to be tired after driving all night. I offer to drive and am surprised at the density of the smoke seen through the car lights. My kids ask why it smells so much like a campfire outside. As we drive off, I explain the situation, hoping that the smoke will improve further down the road.

My mother tells me that because of the fire, all hotels nearby are booked. The only one she could find was a $500 room at a fancy resort almost an hour away. Being a military family, my kids don't fuss over the added distance. They are just excited to see me. We don't arrive in our room until four in the morning. It is difficult for me to sleep. I should be asleep, not tirelessly searching everywhere online for any information about the fire and how it affects the Pacific Crest Trail.

CHAPTER 54

DAY 47 FEMALE FKT ATTEMPT

August 19 & 20 - 3:57 p.m.

3.3 miles / 381 feet

1 hour, 4 minutes

"I know what I have to do but
I don't know if I have the strength to do it."

-Kylo Ren,
Star Wars: The Force Awakens

JUST A FEW HOURS LATER, when morning arrives, I am confused about my next move. I call the Forest Service number posted on the trailhead sign. A woman answers and informs me a massive fire is in the area, and I should contact the Pacific Crest Trail Association (PCTA) to ask for a detour. I search the pcta.org website for information. The page has posted the update, "The Bear Fire, which is part of the North Complex fires, has closed the PCT from Bucks Summit (~mile 1,268) to Quincy (~mile 1,235). The fire is burning along the PCT in the Middle Fork of the Feather River drainage. It is one of many different fires in the area, managed as the North Complex, including the Claremont Fire in the same river drainage." After reading the post, I look at my map to figure out the mileage for southbound travel. Mile 1,235 on the trail is mile 1,385 when heading SOBO, and mile 1,268 is mile 1,418 when heading SOBO.

I message the Pacific Crest Trail Association on Facebook. They quickly respond, telling me they will not be rerouting anyone this year. This means my Fastest Known Time attempt is over. *This can't be it,* I think to myself while staring at the PCTA's response for a reroute. All my hard work and effort gone in a blink of an eye.

I am not ready to throw in the towel just yet. The FKT is out the door, but my desire to finish the trail has only grown. I will skip the thirty-three-mile closed section and pick up at Quincy, where the trail is open. Once the fire is under control, I will come back and re-hike the section I have missed. I look on my Guthook guide and find an area just a few miles up from where the trail is closed.

My family and I leave the hotel by eleven and make the drive to the drop-off. As we drive closer, police officers and fire trucks block the road to Quincy, forcing us to turn around. The fire has spread. Feeling optimistic that the fires will be more in control over the next twenty-four hours, I book another $500 room two hours away. I then decide to hike the area where our hotel is and make up the mileage I will be missing. After two miles of hiking and being able to process the situation fully, I finally conclude that this is stupid. I should be with my kids and enjoying pool time with them.

The following morning, we look out of the resort's window in astonishment. The sky has completely darkened. Smoke has filled the air and has overtaken the sun. The smell of campfire has made its way to our room. Yet, I am still too stubborn to give up, determined to finish what I started. I don't like failing, and I don't like to quit.

We drive 100 miles further towards the trail hoping the air quality will be better, but the situation doesn't improve. The sky still looks hazy, and I know the reality and what I need to do but can't admit it. I turn to my mom, defeated. As though she can read my mind, she says, "It's okay, Jess. I don't think you should continue." We talk about the smoke and the damage it can do to a person. Being a nurse, she has seen it all. The worried look on her face as she tells me I am making the right decision is enough to put a stamp on my journey.

My mom knows me all too well, though. She knows I don't like quitting. She asks if I am okay, and of course, I lie. I am frustrated. In one single moment, the trail and FKT were pulled out from under me, slipping away from my grasp. Still in shock, I don't know what I should be feeling. Should I be angry, upset, sad, or thankful I wasn't in the middle of the fire? Surely there must be a lesson I could learn from this change in events. With every negative thrown my way, I turn the tables and learn from my mistakes. Yet this wasn't something I did or an error I made. I am not quitting because I'm giving up. I am forced to stop and forced to leave. It is out of my control. I am still not ready to let go. I have time left on my hiking permit. I will come back in a few weeks when the fire is under control and finish what I started.

CHAPTER 55

DRIVING HOME

August 21 - 10:00 a.m

0 miles / 0 feet

0 hours, 0 minutes

"When we travel, we always
leave a bit of ourselves behind."
-Daniel Wippert

DURING THE DRIVE HOME, we listen to the news on the radio. We learn the record-breaking heat that forced me to hike at night last week had also brought a wave of dry lightning, the same lightning storms I had been in a few days ago that forced me to hunker down as they passed. According to the news, nearly 12,000 lightning strikes, a historic lightning siege, had devastated California causing about 585 fires. Six of the wildfires would eventually make the top twenty for the largest fires in California history. Four of them ranking in the top ten.

As photos of the fires burning down hundreds of homes are posted all over social media, I begin to feel selfish. I had a plan, but nature had other plans and the end of my PCT journey doesn't compare to what others currently face. I hold back tears after learning about the destroyed homes of people and animals. The land was going up in flames. I have friends in California and begin to message every one of them, making sure they are safe. Over the next few weeks, I monitor the news and locations of the fires. Several are under control, but the air quality is horrible.

After a few hours have passed and I have had some time to cool off and process everything that is happening, I update my status on social media. When I open my Instagram, my cousin's name is at the top list of messages. I open his first. He does not know my status just yet, so I give him an update. His response is both kind and genuine. "I'm happy you decided to make your safety a priority. It is good you made this decision. It may have been hard. Not what you wanted, but there is always a reason the way things turn out." What he writes next will stick with me always. "Stay positive, stay healthy. Lay down tobacco, thanking Mother Earth for keeping you safe and for all the spirit helpers for watching over you. Know where you are today. Call yourself, call out your proper name. You will bring yourself to the present. When we travel, we always leave a bit of ourselves behind. Soon our mind wanders to that place. Lay tobacco down, call yourself after traveling. Then light sweetgrass and smudge off."

His words could not have been more genuine, and I must have read them a thousand times. Only I was coming back in a few weeks and wanted nothing more than to be out still doing what I have grown to love. Bits and pieces of me were scattered along the trail. I am not ready to let go and bring those pieces back. I want my mind to wander back to nature and to the trail. I want to finish what I started. So, I lay tobacco to thank the creator, Mother Earth, and my ancestors for their guidance. However, I am not ready to smudge off the end to my journey just yet.

CHAPTER 56

BACK ON TRAIL

September 5 - 4:00 p.m.

19.9 miles / 2,530 feet

6 hours, 57 minutes

"I have not failed. I've just found
10,000 ways that won't work."

-Thomas Edison

TWO WEEKS HAVE PASSED, and I am even more eager to get back on the trail. We make the trip from Washington State to California for my drop-off. Containing the fires has improved, but some are still not under control, and the air quality depends on the wind conditions. I choose a location fifty-six miles from where I left the trail. It is at mile marker 1,440 and is the closest area on the Pacific Crest Trail that is open. When we make it to Gold Lake, I say my goodbyes to my kids, mom, and dogs, and I am soon on my way. After an hour passes, I realize I had forgotten my trekking poles in the car. I message my mom as soon as I can and ask if she can have Glenna mail them to my next resupply point. My mom tells me she doesn't have to be back to work for a few days and can stay an extra few nights if I want. I agree that it would be great and give her the location to meet me: Highway 49 near Sierra City.

The feeling of being back on the trail is filled with mixed emotions. I am both happy but saddened. I should have been passing this section two weeks ago and finishing my final days of the hike. I should almost be done. It's a little heart-wrenching to think about all the "should haves." I try to focus on being in the moment and not take these miles for granted ever again.

Being able to rest and fatten up for two weeks has strengthened me. I take each climb with ease and gratitude. The trail remains hazy from all of the fires still occurring throughout California. I just hope the air quality improves the further south I head.

By evening, my mother messages that she has made it to our meet-up location. She tells me to be careful because she just saw a bear cross the road. I tell her not to worry since my lights are as bright as the sun and I try to stay loud. By eleven that night, I reach the car. She informs me that because it is Labor Day, she couldn't find a hotel room for the night. They are all booked up. We drive an hour into Truckee in hopes of getting a room there. Still no luck. We end up finding a location near a campground around two in the morning. I set up my tent, sharing it with my son and one dog, Lily. The girls, mom, and older dog, Roxy, sleep in the car.

Chapter 57

Uncertainty

September 6 - 12:33 p.m.

12.57 miles / 2,858 feet

4 hours, 50 minutes

"The only certainty is uncertainty."

-Pliny the Elder

WHEN MORNING ARRIVES, we drive into Truckee for breakfast. My mom agrees to stick around for one more day. I make plans to hike just twelve miles and then be picked up. My Weimaraner, Lily, also joins me for the day. I still have one item left to check off on my bucket list: take a dip in a lake. Washington was too cold, and I was sick in Oregon. I let the opportunity to dunk in each of those states slip by me. I couldn't set an FKT, but I can at least finish one thing I set out to accomplish. Lily and I make our way to the North Yuba River. Lily has never been one to swim. Unlike our Labrador, if there's water, she is nowhere near it. I jump in and take a few strokes out, but the cold takes my breath away. Lily catches me by surprise and follows me, swimming directly behind me. When she has made her way next to me, I grab her and push her back towards shore. She is such a faithful companion. We both exit the water together, dry off, and head back out on the trail.

When we made it a few miles past the trailhead, I let Lily off her leash. She runs a few feet in front of me, then turns back and stares as if trying to say, "C'mon, you slow human." I call her over and give her some leftover bread from this morning's breakfast. She wags her tail and continues running. Lily is three years old. We adopted her last year. She had already been through three owners before us. We knew once we had her, there was no giving her up. Since we got her, she has become a part of the family and has been my best trail running companion. She is fast, fierce, and is always looking out for me. She is the greatest trail buddy anyone could ask for.

After twelve miles of hiking, we sit on a boulder and wait for my mom to arrive. She picks us up before dinner time and takes us to the hotel. When morning comes, there is a change in the wind and another fire in the area. I check the air quality on my phone, and it is far worse today than yesterday. We head back towards the trail, and the smoke worsens.

The unpredictability of where the smoke or fires will go helps me make my final decision. I know what I need to do. To offer more validity towards my choice, I say it aloud, "Yesterday was my last day on the Pacific Crest Trail." I look at the mile marker of where I stopped, mile 1,471.1. Minus the fifty-six miles I skipped to start back up on the trail, that means I completed 1,415 miles and climbed nearly 245,000 feet on the Pacific

Crest Trail. I sit for a while thinking about what I accomplished and am at peace with my decision. I am especially proud I made this decision on my own. I am glad I got to end the trail on a high note with Lily by my side. I know the trail will always be there, and I don't regret trying to come back and finish what I started. It was exactly the closure I needed.

CHAPTER 58

September 7

0 miles

"Wisdom comes alone through suffering."

-Aeschylus

I ACCEPT THAT MY JOURNEY HAS COME TO AN END. I am grateful for all the lessons I have learned. I am also thankful for having the tremendous support of my loving husband, mother, children, family, friends, and even people I have never met.

I learned that no matter how solid you think your plans are, your ability to adapt and face challenges is an essential aspect of thru-hiking. My ending is a great life lesson. It does not do any good to dwell on the negative when things don't go your way. If you do, then you just might miss out on all the good. From the beginning, I knew I was doomed, and yet, I still pushed on. Even though I failed at earning the Fastness Known Time Southbound Record, I was able to live my dream of hiking the trail. Stubbornness, grit, optimism, hope, and probably a bit of stupidity are what got me through and kept me fighting.

The trail gave me clarity and connection. Connection with the creator, the land, and my people. Culture has always been a confusing aspect of my life. I did not go into this thinking how spiritually and culturally connected I would become. I could feel my ancestors' presence protecting and guiding me along the way. I learned more about myself and my beliefs in the past month and a half than I have in my entire life. The trail allowed me to tap into something far greater than what I could ever understand.

I also learned about the kindness of strangers. The world may be full of many bad people, but the amount of kindness I received from trail angels and those following my journey on social media was far beyond what I had ever expected. The trail angels who helped me along the way were genuine and asked for nothing in return. I can't thank them enough.

I also cannot thank my family enough. My husband supported me throughout my entire journey. He has never been the one to turn down my goals or dreams. He has always believed in me, and I am a better person because of him. My mother is also an amazing human being. Since the time I was little, she has always supported my adventurous spirit. No matter how crazy or scared I have made her during this lifetime, she continues to be there. She is the driving force behind who I am.

I am thankful I was given the opportunity to hike the Pacific Crest Trail. I had never imagined it would aid in facing my hidden truths. The wilderness allowed me to begin to accept my demons and open up about what has haunted me for years. It allowed me to grieve. It gave me the strength I never knew I had. I could cry without the fear of someone catching me. It didn't judge. It gave me the freedom I never knew I needed. For once, I accepted what I feared most, my battle with Post Traumatic Stress Disorder. I had been in denial for years, ashamed at what others would think if they knew. I have learned that it is not about them, and my mental health is important. It is essential to try and become a better version of myself. I know I can't erase parts of my past, but I also know I can't let the past determine my future.

Once I finally make it home, I open the drawer to where I have stored the sweet grass given to me by Chief Earl Oldperson. I light it and let the smoke course around my body. I begin to pray. As though a weight has lifted, I feel at peace. Hopefully, I will get another opportunity to hike the Pacific Crest Trail. I want to go back and finish what I started, and if the timing is right, one day I will reattempt the Southbound Fastest Known Time Pacific Crest Trail speed record.

Made in the USA
Middletown, DE
24 March 2023

27608490R00169